DIVINE LAW AND HUMAN NATURE

Or, the first book of *Of the Laws of Ecclesiastical Polity*, Concerning Laws and their Several Kinds in General

By RICHARD HOOKER

Edited/translated by W. Bradford Littlejohn, Brian Marr, and Bradley Belschner

Copyright © 2017 The Davenant Trust

All rights reserved.

ISBN: 0692901000
ISBN-13: 978-0692901007

Front cover image taken from Claude Vignon (1593–1670),
Moses with the Tablets of the Law (Nationalmuseum, Stockholm)

Richard Hooker
by Wenceslaus Hollar

CONTENTS

	Introduction	i
	Notes on Editorial Approach	xv
1	The Reason for Writing this General Discourse	1
2	The Law by which God has from the Beginning Determined to Do all Things	4
3	The Law by which Natural Agents Work	10
4	The Law by which Angels Work	18
5	The Law by which Man is Directed to the Imitation of God	22
6	How Men First Begin to Know the Law they Should Observe	25
7	Man's Will, which Laws of Action are Made to Guide	28
8	Of the Natural Way to Find Out Laws by Reason to Lead the Will to What is Good	33
9	The Advantages of Keeping the Law Taught by Reason	46
10	How Reason Leads Men to Make the Laws by which Political Societies are Governed and to Agree about Laws of Fellowship between Independent Societies	49
11	Why God has made Known in Scripture Supernatural Laws to Direct Men's Steps	64

12	Why so Many Natural Laws and Laws of Reason are Found in Scripture	74
13	The Advantage of Having Such Divine Laws Written	77
14	The Sufficiency of Scripture unto the End for which it was Instituted	80
15	Positive Laws in Scripture, how Some of them are Changeable, and the General Use of Scripture	86
16	Conclusion: How All of This Pertains to the Present Controversy	91

INTRODUCTION

IN THE "Preface to the Preface" which appeared at the beginning of the first volume of our project to modernize or even translate the text of Richard Hooker's remarkable *Lawes of Ecclesiastical Politie*, I outlined the case for undertaking a "translation" of a work originally written in English, and in truly extraordinary English at that. I will not belabor the point by repeating that case here. Let it suffice to make two points.

First, Hooker needs to be read. My conviction on this has grown stronger day by day; nearly every time my colleagues and I meet (three times a week) to work on this project, we find ourselves coming upon a passage that leads us to exclaim, "Dang! People need to hear this!" The current state of our political discourse and profound public confusion even about the meaning of political life; the superficial and fragmented character of our church life, with intellectual vapidity characterizing most liberal and moderate Christianity and narrow dogmatisms and biblicisms afflicting most conservative Christianity; the parlous state of Christian undergraduate and seminary education—all cry out for a blast of wisdom from the past, and I would argue, for the judicious Hooker's distinctive brand of wisdom in particular.

Second, even among professional Hooker scholars, there is a recognition that with the passage of time and the dumbing down of our language, Hooker has become almost inaccessible to the layman, and to the clergyman too for that matter. If people are to read Hooker again today, he needs to be translated into something approximating the contemporary English tongue, with sentences of a shortness and simplicity that make at least some concessions to mere mortals' attention spans—without sacrificing overmuch the profundity and elegance of the original. While the sentences in this paragraph may not inspire much confidence that *I* should be entrusted with that responsibility, I hope and trust that you will find in the pages that follow that the luminosity and clarity of Hooker's thought is matched in at least some measure by luminous, clear, and crisp prose. Working sentence by sentence and paragraph by paragraph with my colleagues Brian Marr and Brad Belschner, I believe we have succeeded in reproducing as closely as possible the substance (and indeed where possible the phrasing) of Hooker's thought, while minimizing as much as possible barriers to understanding. To be sure, this translation should not be treated as a substitute for the original. Hooker's intricate sentence structures are self-conscious and in many cases play a key role in conveying meaning and rhetorical effect. Our hope is that readers may find these editions an accessible point of entry, and then go on to engage the genuine article in due course, experiencing in the process some taste of the illumination and edification it has been our blessing to experience in the course of this project.

INTRODUCTION

In this second volume of our project, we come to the work that Hooker is perhaps most renowned for. Here, in Book I, he offers a sweeping overview of his theology of law, *law* being that order and measure by which God governs the universe and by which all creatures, and humans above all, conduct their lives and affairs. In an age when Scripture has come under attack, so that the seriousness of one's commitment to the Christian faith is often simply equated with one's fidelity to Scripture, Hooker's seeming attempt to relativize the role of Scripture may cause eyebrows to furrow in suspicion. In carving out a role for natural reason and human law, is he not perhaps an early apostle of the Enlightenment and modern secularism? If not, perhaps he is at least a representative of that type that appears in every age, the lukewarm spokesman for worldly wisdom who advises his fellow Christians about the need for moderation in all things, even in obeying God's Word. So some readers of Hooker—and many more who have not bothered to read him—have imagined through the centuries.

But such a reading betrays the very confusion that Hooker warns against. As he says of his opponents in the concluding chapter of this book, "they rightly maintain that God must be glorified in all things and that men's actions cannot glorify Him unless they are based on His laws. However, they are mistaken to think that the only law which God has appointed for this is Scripture." Rather, even "what we do naturally, such as breathing, sleeping, and moving, displays the glory of God just as natural agents do, even if we do not have any express purpose in mind, but act for the most part unconsciously" (I.16.5; p.

95).¹ In fact, Hooker compellingly argued throughout his *Laws* that it was precisely those who most exalted Scripture as God's only revelation to us who were at most risk of secularizing. For this theory, however much it might attempt to find Scriptural teaching for any and every matter, must admit that when there was a matter where such teaching could not be found, here was an area left entirely to our own wits, without a ray of divine wisdom. But we must not so limit the scope of divine wisdom, argued Hooker.

C.S. Lewis, who revered Hooker as both one of the greatest of English prose writers and one of the great theologians of the Christian tradition, wrote that "there could be no deeper mistake" than to think that Hooker was disposed "to secularize." On the contrary,

> few model universes are more filled—one might say, more drenched—with Deity than his. "All things that are of God" (and only sin is not) "have God in them and he them in himself likewise" yet "their substance and his wholly differeth" (V.56.5). God is unspeakably transcendent; but also unspeakably immanent. It is this conviction which enables Hooker, with no anxiety, to resist any inaccurate claim that is made for revelation against reason, Grace against Nature, the spiritual against the secular.²

---

[1] Quotations from Hooker in this Introduction are taken from our modernized text (accompanied by page references to this volume) when they come from Book I unless otherwise specified; when from later books, as in the case of this quotation, we have simply updated the spelling.

[2] C.S. Lewis, *Oxford History English Literature in the Sixteenth Century*,

INTRODUCTION

Throughout his work, but especially in this foundational Book I of the *Laws*, Hooker sought to apply the Thomistic dictum that "grace does not destroy nature, but perfects it." That is to say, he insisted that grace enabled human reason, and human political community, to achieve its natural potential, to function rightly within its own limitations, and to point beyond itself to the operations of grace that transcended those limitations. The supernatural law of Scripture, then, must not "clean have abrogated...the law of nature" (II.8.6), as it seemed to do in some forms of puritanism. Rather, Hooker insisted that regarding matters of temporal life, Scripture would serve to enrich, illuminate, clarify, and apply the law of nature, straightening and sharpening a bent and blunt tool, but not replacing it.[3]

Lest the allusion to Thomism suggest in the minds of some readers the old illusion that we find in Hooker a wistful glance back to the Catholic past and an uneasiness with Protestantism's abandonment of the medieval scholastic legacy, a mountain of recent publications should suffice to destroy that nonsense. While Hooker might have

---

Excluding Drama, vol. 5 of *The Oxford History of English Literature* (Oxford: Clarendon Press, 1954), 459.

[3] Hooker's approach here is remarkably similar to that of his contemporary Franciscus Junius, who would write, "And therefore with respect to the laws by which nature itself is preserved and renewed, grace restores those that have been lost, renews those that have been corrupted, and teaches those that are unknown" (Franciscus Junius the Elder, *De Politiae Mosis Observatione*, 2nd ed. [Lugduni Batavorum: Christopher Guyot, 1602], 12; *The Mosaic Polity: Sources in Early Modern Economics, Ethics, and Law*, trans. Todd M. Rester, and ed. Andrew M. McGinnis [Grand Rapids: Christian's Library Press, 2015]; see further my essay, "Cutting Through the Fog in the Channel: Hooker, Junius, and a Reformed Theology of Law," in *Richard Hooker and Reformed Orthodoxy*, ed. W. Bradford Littlejohn and Scott N. Kindred Barnes [Gottingen: Vandenhoeck and Ruprecht, 2017], 221-240).

been among the very greatest of Protestant natural law theorists, he was hardly unique in his basic principles, and the Thomistic dictum can be found in both spirit and letter in many of his Reformed contemporaries. The time is long past when Protestants need to choose between stubbornly priding themselves on their allegiance to Barth or Van Til, or sheepishly cracking open the *Summa* in their closets. We have in our tradition some of the finest expressions of a theology of Scripture and reason together, special revelation and natural revelation, divine law and human nature, that have ever been penned, and it is high time to bring them into the pulpits and into the classrooms. The current volume is one attempt to make this happen.[4]

To aid the reader for whom these various categories of divine and human, natural and supernatural law are unfamiliar, the following summary may be helpful.[5]

Hooker begins his *apologia* not with the divine law of Scripture, as a Puritan might, or the laws of England, as a conformist might be tempted to, but with the primordial source from which both ultimately derive, "the eternal law," which is, in Hooker's words "laid up in the bosom of God" (I.3.1, original wording). Indeed, God himself oper-

---

[4] Another worthy endeavor along similar lines, to which we are deeply indebted, is the ongoing *Sources in Early Modern Economics, Ethics, and Law* series currently being produced by Christian's Library Press.

[5] For a fuller version of the summary below, see ch. 6 of my *Peril and Promise of Christian Liberty* (Grand Rapids, William B. Eerdmans, 2017); see also Cargill Thompson, "Philosopher of the 'Politic Society'," in *Studies in the Reformation: Luther to Hooker*, ed. C. W. Dugmore (London: Athlone Press, 1980), 150–60; Joan O'Donovan, *Theology of Law and Authority in the English Reformation* (Grand Rapids: Eerdmans, 1991), 137–42; W.J. Torrance Kirby, "Reason and Law," in *A Companion to Richard Hooker*, ed. W.J. Torrance Kirby (Leiden: Brill, 2008), 251–71.

ates according to this law, for law is intrinsic to being itself:

> All things that exist work in a way that is neither unnatural nor random. Nor do they ever work without a preconceived end or goal. And the end which they work for is not achieved unless the work is also fit to achieve it by, for different ends require different modes of working. Therefore, we define a *Law* as that which determines what kind of work each thing should do, how its power should be restrained, and what form its work should take (I.2.1; p. 4).

In the case of God, we do not say that the eternal law governs his being, but that his being *is* this law (I.2.2), a law that encompasses every kind of law, inasmuch as God's operations encompass all that is; it is "the order which God before all ages has set down with Himself for Himself to do all things by" (I.2.6; p. 9). Here Hooker introduces a distinction unique to his exposition, notably departing from Aquinas by describing this order as the "eternal law"; the second kind of law is "that which He has established for all his different creatures to obey" (I.3.1; p. 10). By this distinction, he seeks to steer clear of the idea that God's will is arbitrary, emphasizing instead the law-likeness and rationality of God's eternal decrees. But at the same time he seeks to preserve a sharp Creator/creature distinction, showing that although united in God, these decrees from our creaturely standpoint remain distinct from his revealed will, and thus inscrutable to us.

Having safeguarded the inscrutability of the first eternal law, Hooker turns his exclusive attention in what follows to the second, which although one in itself, unfolds itself in different forms according to its different agents. Hooker summarizes succinctly:

> When applied to natural agents, we call it the law of *nature*; when applied to the rule which Angels behold and obey without swerving, we call it the heavenly or *celestial* law; when applied to the law which binds reasonable creatures in such a way that they can plainly perceive it, we call it the law of *reason*; when applied to that which binds them in such a way that only special revelation can make it known, we call it the *divine* law; when applied to those laws which are derived from both reason and revelation as prudential judgments, we call it *human* law (I.3.1; p. 11).

Hooker has relatively little to say about the *celestial* law, given how little of it is disclosed to us in Scripture, and indeed his chief interest, with the rest of the Christian natural law tradition, is with the "law of reason," governing as it does our moral actions. However, it is important to grasp the larger cosmology within which this concept is grounded. For Hooker, as for the whole medieval world which had not yet passed away by 1600, every order of creature is drawn into motion by seeking the perfection that belongs to it, a perfection that is its own unique mode of imitating the divine perfection. Plants do this in a very limited way, animals in a more perfect way, human beings by the much higher gift of reason, and angels the most perfectly of all. "The law of reason," then, is not the autonomous reason of the later Enlightenment, but the distinctive mode of human striving toward God; we, unlike lower creatures, are called upon to reflect on, discern, and actively pursue the goodness proper to our natures. Man thus seeks not only after the perfections proper to all creatures, but to further perfections "which are desired for the mere sake of knowing them.... [M]an, uniquely among the creatures of this world, aspires to the greatest conformity with God by pursuing the knowledge of truth and by growing in the exercise of virtue" (I.5.3; p. 23).

By recognizing those goods which constitute the perfection of our nature and gaining experience in pursuing them, we derive maxims and axioms as a guide to right conduct. Of course, these are not always easy to discern, since there are a multitude of possible goods to choose from, and we often choose a less over a greater, or a faulty route to a genuine good. Nevertheless, "Every good that concerns us is evident enough that, if we diligently consider it by reason, we cannot fail to recognize it" (I.7.7; p. 32). Therefore, although Hooker has no illusions about the power and prevalence of widely engrained error, he does not believe that it can ever become universal. Universal consensus, then, must be taken as a token of truth, indeed, "as the judgment of God Himself, since what all men at all times have come to believe must have been taught to them by Nature, and since God is Nature's author, her voice is merely His instrument" (I.8.3; p. 35). Natural reason, Hooker believes, following Romans 1, can perceive the being, power, and fatherhood of God, and can deduce thereby such rules as "'in all things we go about, his aid is to be craved' and 'He cannot have sufficient honor done unto Him, but the utmost of that we can do to honor Him we must do'" (I.8.7; p. 39).[6] The latter of these, he says, is the same as the first great commandment that Jesus gives

---

[6] Hooker is quoting here from Plato's *Timaeus* and Aristotle's *Nicomachean Ethics*.

us—that we must love God with all our hearts. Moreover, by discerning the natural equality of all humans, we will necessarily recognize that one cannot expect to receive any greater good from one's fellows than that which one gives unto them, and can expect to suffer from them in proportion to that which one causes them to suffer; this leads to the principle of the second great commandment, that we must love our neighbors as ourselves.

Before treating of "the divine law" of Scripture, as we might expect him to, Hooker follows his discussion of the law of reason with a discussion of human law, reflecting his Aristotelian conviction that the latter is the chief means by which the general principles of the former are rendered concrete. Human law thus exists to remedy a deficiency in the law of reason, its lack of precision, since disagreement becomes more and more likely the more we descend from the general to the particular, as well as the fact that the law of reason does not usually serve as a sufficient motivation toward virtue. Human law is more than mere rational deliberation about what the law of reason requires in relation to a concrete problem; deliberation can do no more than provide maxims of prudent action for private individuals. Human law has a necessarily *political* dimension; it is law promulgated and in some sense enforced for a community of men and women bound together by compact, by representatives authorized to act on behalf of the whole. Within this section, Hooker draws attention to a fact that is central to his argument throughout the *Lawes*: the vast diversity, and constant mutability, of human societies and circumstances. This diversity calls for great variety in the proper forms of human law, notwithstanding the original unity of its principles in the law of reason.

INTRODUCTION

What, then, of divine law? We might be forgiven at this point for imagining that Hooker has indeed provided us with a robust naturalism, attributing an autonomy and self-sufficiency to the law of reason (and its applications in the form of human law) that would leave little need for revelation within this-worldly affairs. Hooker, however, has much to say about the need for revelation in chapters 11 and 12 of this book.

In this argument, he establishes three things: First, nature and reason cannot be autonomous in the sense of encompassing their own end; nature cannot be considered a self-enclosed compartment, nor can reason be satisfied merely with the task of investigating creation, but our souls *by nature* long subconsciously for union with God. Second, nature and reason cannot be autonomous in the sense of being capable, on their own, of reaching this final, supernatural end. On this point, Hooker is particularly nuanced, attributing most of this incapacity to the reality of sin, but acknowledging a dependence on divine grace even in the state of innocence. Third, nature and reason cannot be autonomous even in the sense of being perfectly adequate to the task of discerning and reaching man's natural ends, without use of revelation. This last point warrants particular attention.

To be sure, Hooker has a great deal to say in praise of reason's ability to guide us in such endeavors. After all, God's wisdom comes to us in many ways—from "the sacred books of Scripture...in Nature's glorious works...by a spiritual influence from above...through experience and practice in the world"—all of which are to be respected and valued in their particular place: "We may not so in any one special kind admire her, that we disgrace her in any other; but let all her ways be according unto their place and degree adored" (II.1.4). However, Hooker does not in fact think that the law of reason has no use of scriptural illumination within the realm of natural duties, nor is he dismissive of the effects of the Fall, as often charged. On the contrary, he is careful to enumerate the limitations of natural reason not once but twice within these chapters. In chapter 8, where he provides his first survey of the law of reason, he qualifies its capabilities with three caveats. First, he says, it is not that the law of reason is *in fact* known to all men, but that it is such that "once the law of reason is described, no one can reject it as unreasonable or unjust" and such that "there is nothing in it that any man with the full use of his wits and in possession of sound judgment will not find out if he searches diligently enough" (I.8.9; p. 42). They are in themselves knowable by all men, but that does not mean that a lack of such labor and travail may not leave many in ignorance of them. He returns to this theme in I.12, saying that for this reason, "the application of the laws of nature to difficult particular cases is of great value for our instruction" (I.12.1; p. 74). And when we are vexed with doubt as to whether we have determined and applied the law of reason correctly, the clear divine authority of these specific pronouncements is a great help to us. Hooker considers this a limitation of our "original" (i.e., unfallen), not "depraved" nature, though sin exacerbates this considerably, so that "when it comes to particular applications of this law, so far has our natural understanding been darkened that at times whole nations have been unable to recognize even gross iniquity as sin" (I.12.2; p. 75).

Indeed, this is because of a second limitation that sin

INTRODUCTION

particularly introduces, that of "perverted and wicked customs," which, "perhaps beginning with a few and spreading to the multitude, and then continuing for a long time…may be so strong that they smother the light of our natural understanding" (I.8.11; p. 43). By this means, it would seem, many of the key principles of the law of reason could become thoroughly obscured by sinful man. Related to this is Hooker's discussion of our fallen propensity to "we are inclined to flatter ourselves and to learn as little about our defects as possible" (I.12.2; p. 75) so that we need to be told where our faults are and how they are to be fixed. Our nature has been distorted by sin, but that very sin keeps us from so much as recognizing the deformity; hence divine law comes to our aid and points it out to us. An example of this is the Sermon on the Mount, where Jesus reveals even secret concupiscence to be sin, where we might have deceived ourselves into imagining that the natural law required only outward purity (I.12.2).

The third qualification is that the faculty of reason always depends upon the "aid and concurrence" of God, which, should we make God withdraw His aid, then we can expect only the darkness described in Romans 1,

> men who have been blessed with the light of reason will walk "in the vanity of their mind, being darkened in their understanding, alienated from the life of God, because of the ignorance that is in them, because of the hardening of their heart" (I.8.11; p. 45).

After the Fall, then, although God continues to extend enough of his favor to most men to enable them to discern some knowledge of moral laws, their grasp is no longer clear and reliable, particularly when we move beyond natural law's first principles to second-order deductions. Hence, there seems to be the need for a supplementary source of revelation that will pierce through the self-imposed darkness of sin.

For all these reasons, then, we may be immensely grateful to God for providing in Scripture not merely a guide to the path of salvation, but considerable instruction in natural moral duties as well. Hooker summarizes the relationship of natural and divine law at the end of Book I:

> The law of reason teaches men in part how to honor God as their Creator, but we are taught by divine law how to glorify Him in such a way that He may be our everlasting Savior. This divine law both makes certain the truth of the law of reason and supplies what is lacking in it; therefore in moral actions, the divine law greatly helps the law of reason in guiding man's life, but in supernatural matters, it alone guides us (I.16.5).

NOTES ON EDITORIAL APPROACH

MANY OF the following notes will be familiar to readers of our first volume, *Radicalism*, but if you are curious as to just how we set about "translating" a book from English into English, or are seeking for proof of why it was necessary, read on.

Modernizing Hooker's prose was a complex task, certainly more complicated than updating a few archaic words and breaking apart a few lengthy sentences. Hooker's sentences are not just lengthy; rather, his syntax itself is often dense and unwieldy, even by 16th century standards. Much of this is intentional, perhaps, and helps convey Hooker's meaning, but it is so challenging for most modern readers that many sentences required syntactical re-working of some kind. Hooker's idioms and turns of phrase are also frequently archaic or rhetorically elevated in Shakespearean ways that can be obscure to the modern reader, so our vocabulary updates were extensive. Our revision is therefore a deep and pervasive one, with the outcome being more of a translation than a modernization.

Our translation method was a simple one. First, Brian Marr would privately read and carefully re-write Hooker's prose from scratch, translating Hooker's meaning and prose into modern parlance as best as he was able. Second, at a later date the three of us—Brian Marr, Bradford Littlejohn, and Bradley Belschner—would sit down and meet to read the prose aloud, beginning with Hooker's original and comparing it to Brian's translation. In this way we worked through Hooker's work, sentence by sentence, paragraph by paragraph, with an eye towards style, subtle connotations in the text, and key terms in Hooker's argument. It was a laborious process, and often the final version would end up looking markedly different than Brian's first draft. Finally, we read aloud through the entire modernized version on its own, our ears listening for any needless impediments to clarity or readability.

Since our goal in this "translation" process was to render Hooker's prose easily accessible to a modern audience, we adopted a method that in traditional terms would be considered dynamic rather than literal. The goal was to convey Hooker's *meaning* as accurately and intuitively as possible to a modern audience. We felt free to use reasonably modern colloquialisms, though we also eschewed any words or phrases that smacked entirely of the current century. We often found that such phrases, transparently modern as they were, drew attention to themselves rather than to the underlying text. This defeated one of our main goals, which was to remove as many distractions as possible from the meaning that Hooker was trying to convey, allowing it to shine through without occasioning the reader any uncomfortable pauses. Indeed, when in doubt, we erred in favor of what might be a more 19th- than 21st-century English style, when the latter was so clearly incongruous with the subject matter to feel out of place. For this reason, there were certain conventions that we did not seek to bring into line with common 21st-century standards, most notable among them Hooker's convention of using masculine nouns and pronouns where gender-neutral ones are now widely preferred. To change his "man" to "humanity" or his "he" to "he or she" would have been so incongruous with the habits of his age as to have drawn needless attention to itself.

For devotees of Hooker's original, let it not be thought that we needlessly flattened out his often noble rhetoric and remarkable turns of phrase into a bland, flat, and simplistic sentence structure. On the contrary, if the basic phrasing and rhetorical cadence of the original could be retained without great loss of comprehensibility, we did our utmost to preserve it. Some famous and luminous passages we left virtually untouched. Any reader of Hooker cannot but come away with an enhanced ear for the English language, for words that sound crisp or sonorous and those that are flat and dull. Thus, even when it was clear to us that we would have to find some more modern synonym for a now-obsolete term, we often puzzled long over a single word until we found the one that did the job without detracting from the elegance of the original.

Examples of Changes

Below are a few examples to give a sense of cases when extensive reworking was sometimes necessary, of when a few judicious changes did the trick, and of when almost no change at all was called for.

Here is a passage where length of sentences, complexity of syntax, archaism of language, and indeed archaism of thought all conspire to render comprehension quite difficult for the contemporary reader:

> The knowledge of that which man is in reference unto himself, and other things in relation unto man, I may justly term the mother of all those principles, which are as it were edicts, statutes, and decrees, in that Law of Nature, whereby human actions are framed. First therefore having observed that the best things, where they are not hindered, do still produce the best operations (for which cause, where many things are to concur unto one effect, the best is in all congruity of reason to guide the residue, that it prevailing most, the work principally done by it may have greatest perfection), when hereupon we come to observe in ourselves, of what excellency our souls are in comparison of our bodies, and the diviner part in relation unto the baser of our souls; seeing that all these concur in producing human actions, it cannot be well unless the chiefest do command and direct the rest (I.8.6, original, spelling modernized).

> Knowledge of both what man is in himself and what he is in relation to all other things is the mother of all the edicts, statutes, and decrees in the law of nature, by which human actions are guided. When the best things rule, the best things follow. Thus, when we see how much worthier our souls are than our bodies, and the more divine part of our souls than the baser part, it is clear that all is not well unless the greater commands and directs the lesser (our version, p. 38).

You will note that here, as often in such cases, our modernization resulted in a significant shortening; indeed, there were a number of places where strict application of Strunk and White's Rule #17, "Omit needless words," required some pruning of Hookerian prolixity.

For an example of where more minor changes were sufficient, consider this passage:

> And lest appetite in the use of food should lead us beyond that which is meet, we owe in this case obedience to that law of Reason, which teacheth mediocrity in meats and drinks. The same things divine law teacheth also, as at large we have shewed it doth all parts of moral duty (I.16.7, original, spelling modernized).

Words such as "mediocrity," "meet," and "shewed" obviously weren't going to do, and the syntax of the second clause in particular was awkward. But extensive reconstructive surgery was unnecessary:

> Furthermore, lest appetite for food should lead us to take more than is necessary, we ought to obey the law of Reason, which teaches moderation regarding food and drink. The divine law of Scripture teaches the same thing, as we have previously shown it does in all parts of moral duty (our version, p. 98).

And then there are cases where Hooker's prose is so elegant and luminous that to undertake more than very minor changes would be sacrilege, not to mention superfluous:

> Dangerous it were for the feeble brain of man

> to wade far into the doings of the Most High; whom although to know be life, and joy to make mention of his name; yet our soundest knowledge is to know that we know him not as indeed he is, neither can know him: and our safest eloquence concerning him is our silence, when we confess without confession that his glory is inexplicable, his greatness above our capacity and reach. He is above, and we upon earth; therefore it behoveth our words to be wary and few. (I.2.2, original, spelling modernized)

> It is dangerous for the feeble mind of man to wade too far into the doings of the Most High. Although it is life to know Him and joy to mention His name, our surest knowledge is that we do not know Him as He truly is, nor can we; our safest eloquence is our silence, confessing without confession that His glory is inexplicable and His greatness above our capacity and reach. He is above, and we are on earth; therefore let our words be wary and few (our version, p. 5).

Textual Notes

The foundation text for Hooker's *Laws* is widely available, and a free copy is available online at the "Online Library of Liberty" (URL: http://oll.libertyfund.org/titles/hooker-the-works-of-richard-hooker-vol-1). This represents a digitization of the 7th edition of Keble's 1832 edition of Hooker's *Works*, revised by the Very Rev. R.W. Church and the Rev. F. Paget in 3 volumes (Oxford: Clarendon Press, 1888).

EDITORIAL APPROACH

The section numbers noted in parentheses reflect the "paragraph" numbers provided by John Keble in his 1832 edition, which have been adopted as standard in all subsequent editions of Hooker's work. You will note that we also sometimes included additional paragraph breaks within these numbered sections, here too following the precedent established by the edition on the Online Library of Liberty, as we found that more frequent paragraph breaks improved readability. We found it most helpful to retrieve citations from A.S. McGrade's new Oxford University Press edition (*Of the Laws of Ecclesiastical Polity: A Critical Edition with Modern Spelling*), and are very grateful to Prof. McGrade for his labors in providing full citations whenever possible from Hooker's original cryptic notes.

Please note that double quotation marks do not necessarily imply verbatim quotations; Cartwright and other 16th-century English quotations are quite challenging, so they are modernized like Hooker. Sometimes Hooker summarizes rather than quotes greats such as Plato, Aristotle, and Aquinas; for this we have used single quotation marks. In a few cases where Hooker quoted loosely from Scripture or an ancient source, or used his own idiosyncratic translation, we chose to follow (and as necessary, modernize) his version rather than quoting from a standard modern translation. However, our general rule, for quotations of non-English texts, was to use a standard modern translation and reference it accordingly, though occasionally we translated from the Latin or Greek ourselves. Likewise, all scripture quotations are from the American Standard Version, and all Apocryphal quotations from the Revised Standard Version, unless otherwise noted.

We have tried to be very sparse in making any editorial interjections beyond what is strictly necessary, but you will find a few places where we found an explanatory note in order, without which Hooker's meaning was likely to remain opaque to most readers. In a single case, which we have highlighted, an explanatory footnote was original to Hooker.

One final note: attentive readers may note that the font and some aspects of formatting have been altered from our first volume of this project, *Radicalism*. While perfect consistency from volume to volume would indeed be ideal, there is no virtue in stubbornly persisting in imperfection when improvements recommend themselves, and we believe most readers will find this volume an aesthetic improvement on the first.

1
THE REASON FOR WRITING THIS GENERAL DISCOURSE

(1.) WHOEVER wants to persuade the multitude that they are not as well governed as they should be will never lack a sympathetic audience, since everyone can recognize the obvious problems in any kind of government, but they rarely have as much insight into the innumerable hidden obstacles which inevitably hinder the business of governing. Thus, those who bewail the current state of affairs are esteemed to be the champions of the people and men of independent thought, and under this guise whatever they say is accepted without question. Whatever their speech lacks in substance is supplied by people's willingness to believe it. On the other hand, those of us who would defend the status quo are quickly judged as mere time-servers or boot-lickers of the establishment, and people will stop up their ears against our arguments before they even hear them.

(2.) Therefore, much of what we are about to say may seem tedious, obscure, dark, and intricate. Many feel themselves at liberty to talk about the truth, even though they have never plumbed the depths from which it springs and, when they are led there, they quickly get tired because they are being taken off the beaten paths they have trod so often. However, this must not stop the argument from going where the subject demands that it go, whether or not everyone likes it. Anyone for whom this argument is too complex can save themselves the trouble and stop reading now. If anyone thinks it too obscure, they should remember that often in both works of art and in works of nature the most important things are not necessarily the things immediately visible to our eyes. We may admire houses for their stateliness, trees for their beauty, but the foundations which bear up the one, and the roots which nourish the other both lie hidden under the earth. When we need to uncover them, it is not necessarily pleasant, either for those who do it or for those who watch it happening. In just the same way, all who live under good laws may enjoy them and benefit from them with delight and comfort, even if most do not know the grounds or reasons for their goodness. However, when people cease to obey the laws, claiming that they are corrupt and wicked, it becomes necessary to uncover their foundations and roots. Since we are not very accustomed to this, whenever we sit down and do it, it is going to be more needful than enjoyable, and the matters we discuss, because they are so new, will seem dark, complicated, and unfamiliar at first. It is for this reason that throughout this work I have tried to make every premise support what follows after it and to make every conclusion shed further light on what came before. So if men suspend their judgments while we go through these first more general arguments until it is clear where they lead, what might seem to be dark at first will turn out to be quite apparent, just as the later specific determinations will seem much stronger on the basis of what came before.

(3.) The Laws of the Church which have guided us for so many years in the exercise of the Christian religion and the service of the true God, as well as in our rites, customs, and orders of Church government—all these things are being called into question. We are accused of refusing to have Jesus Christ rule over us and of willfully casting His statutes behind our backs and hating to be reformed and made subject to the scepter of His discipline! Behold, for this reason we offer the laws that govern our lives to the trial and judgment of the whole world. We heartily beseech Almighty God, whom we desire to serve according to His own will, that, laying aside all partiality, both we and others will have eyes to see and hearts to embrace what is most acceptable in His sight.

Since we are arguing about the quality of our laws, we cannot make a better beginning than by asking about the nature of law itself, and in particular about that law from which all good laws flow: the law by which God eternally works. Moving on from this law to the law of Nature and then to the law of Scripture, we will have a much easier time once we come to the particular controversies and questions that we have in hand.

2
THE LAW BY WHICH GOD HAS FROM THE BEGINNING DETERMINED TO DO ALL THINGS

(1.) ALL THINGS that exist work in a way that is neither unnatural nor random. Nor do they ever work without a preconceived end or goal. And the end which they work for is not achieved unless the work is also fit to achieve it by, for different ends require different modes of working.

Therefore, we define a *Law* as that which determines what kind of work each thing should do, how its power should be restrained, and what form its work should take. No end could ever be reached unless the means by which it was reached were regular; that is to say, unless the means were suitable, fitting, and appropriate to their end according to a principle, rule, or law. This is true in the first place even of the workings of God Himself.

(2.) All things work, in their own way, according to a law. Nearly everything works according to a law subject to some superior, who has authored it; only the works and operations of God have Him as both their worker and as their law. The very being of God is a sort of law to His working, for the perfection that God is, gives perfection to what God does. The natural, necessary, and internal operations of God—the begetting of the Son and the proceeding of the Spirit—are far beyond the scope of this book. For our purposes, we need only note those operations that begin and continue by the voluntary choice of God who has eternally decreed when and how they should be, and that this eternal decree is what we call an *eternal law*.

It is dangerous for the feeble mind of man to wade too far into the doings of the Most High. Although it is life to know Him and joy to mention His name, our surest knowledge is that we do not know Him as He truly is, nor can we; our safest eloquence is our silence, confessing without confession that His glory is inexplicable and His greatness above our capacity and reach. He is above, and we are on earth; therefore let our words be wary and few.

Our God is one, or rather He is Oneness itself, a unity which has nothing in itself but itself, not consisting of many things, as everything else does. In this essential Unity of God, a hypostatic Trinity subsists in a way that far exceeds the imagination of men. The external operations of God in time and history are such that, even though He is one, each hypostasis does something particular and appropriate. For since they are Three and subsist in the essence of one Deity, it can truly be said that all things are from the Father, by the Son, and through the Holy Spirit. What the Son hears from the Father, and what the Spirit receives from the Father and the Son, we come to receive at the hands of the Spirit (John 16:13-15), and therefore He is the last and nearest to us in order, although in power He is equal to the Second and First.

(3.) Even wise and learned pagans acknowledged that there must be some First Cause, upon which the existence of everything else depends. Nor do they call this cause anything other than an Agent, that is, something that knows what it does and why it does it, and does so according to a certain order or law. Homer, for instance, says that Zeus accomplished his counsel[1] and Hermes Trismegistus admits the same when he says that the demiurge made all the world, not by hands, but by reason.[2] The same is confessed by Anaxagoras and Plato who call the Maker of the whole world a rational worker, and the Stoics, although they thought that the First Cause was fire, also affirmed that the fire, having art, followed a certain course in the making of the world.[3] All these admit that this First Cause took *counsel*, or followed *reason*, or observed a *certain course*. In other words, constant order and law is kept, which order must be its own author. If this were not the case, then it would have to be directed by some worthier or higher cause, and would by definition not be a First Cause. Since it is the first, it alone can be the author of that law according to which it freely acts.

God therefore is a law both to Himself and to everything else. To Himself He is a law in all those things which our Savior speaks of, saying, "My Father worketh even until

---

[1] Homer, *Iliad* 1.5.

[2] Hermes Trismegistus, *The Cup or Monad* 1. Cf. *The Corpus Hermeticum*, trans. G. Mead (United States of America: IAP, 2009), 29, which translates it as "With Reason…not with hands, did the World-maker make the universal World."

[3] *Ioannis Stobaeus Anthologium*, ed. Curt Wachsmuth and Otto Hense, 5 vols. (1884-1912; Berlin: Weidmanns, 1958], 1:37.

now, and I work" (Jn. 5:17). God works nothing without cause. He does all things with some end in mind, and the end for which each are done is the reason He acts. He would never have created woman unless he saw that it would not be good unless she were created. "It is not good that the man should be alone; I will make him a help meet for him" (Gen. 2:18). God only does those things which to leave undone would not be good.

One might ask why, even though God has infinite power, the effects of that power are limited as we see they are. This is because He works toward a certain end and by a certain law which constrains the effects of His power so that it does not work infinitely but only as much as necessary to reach that end: "all things well" (Wisd. 8:1), all in a decent and comely manner, all "by measure and number and weight" (Wisd. 11:20).

(4.) The general end for which God works all things in time is the exercise of His most glorious and abundant excellence. This abundant excellence shows itself in variety, which is why Scripture so often speaks of God's "riches" (cf. Eph. 1:7; Phil. 4:19; Col. 2:3); "The Lord has made everything for Himself" (Prov. 16:4),[4] not because they can add anything to Him, but so that in all things he might show His beneficence and grace.

We might not be able to tell the exact reason for every one of God's actions, and therefore we cannot always give a full account of His works. Nonetheless, every finite work of God has some reason or purpose behind it, since some law has been imposed on it; if there were no law, the work

---

[4] KJV is used here, since it is closer to the original translation.

would have to be infinite, just as the worker Himself is.

(5.) Therefore those who think that God acts without any other cause than His bare will are greatly mistaken. Again, we will not always know the reason, but it is most unreasonable to imagine there is no reason, since He works all things, not only according to His own will, but "after the counsel of His will" (Eph. 1:11). Whatever is done with counsel or wise forethought must have some reason behind it, even if the reason is in some cases so secret that it makes a man stand amazed, as the Apostle Paul did: "O the depth of the riches both of the wisdom and the knowledge of God! How unsearchable are his judgments, and his ways past tracing out!" (Rom. 11:33). That eternal law which God Himself is to Himself and by which He works all things which have their origin in Him; that law on which the countenance of wisdom shines and says, "The Lord possessed me in the beginning of His way, before His works of old" (Prov. 8:22); that law which is the pattern for the making of the world and the compass by which to guide it; that law which is of God and with Him everlastingly; again I say, that law whose author and sustainer is the God who is blessed forever, how should either man or angel be ever able to perfectly behold? The book of this law we are neither able nor worthy to open and look into. The little which we barely glimpse, we admire; the rest in devout ignorance we humbly and meekly adore.

(6.) Since He works according to this law, and "of Him, and through Him, and unto Him, are all things" (Rom. 11:36), though confusion and disorder may appear to be in this world, "since a good governor does regulate the universe, do not doubt that all things are rightly done."[5] He is so good that he does not violate His own law, a law than which nothing can be more absolute, perfect, or just.

The law by which God works is eternal, and therefore it is utterly immutable. This is why, since part of that law has been revealed in God's promises to do good for mankind, the Apostle Paul declares that God is just as likely to "deny Himself" and not be God as to fail to carry them out (2 Tim. 2:13). He also says that the counsel of God is similarly a thing unchangeable (Heb. 6:17); the counsel of God and the law of God which we now describe are one and the same.

The freedom of God is in no way diminished by this, since God freely and voluntarily binds Himself to this law. We may therefore call this the *eternal* law, since it is the *order which God before all ages has set down with Himself for Himself to do all things by*.

---

[5] Boethius, *Boethius: Tractates, On the Consolation of Philosophy*, trans. H. F. Stewart, E.K. Rand, and S.J. Tester, Loeb Classical Library 74 (1918; Cambridge, MA: Harvard University Press, 1973), 355 [*Consolation of Philosophy* 4.4].

3
THE LAW BY WHICH NATURAL AGENTS WORK

(1.) I AM AWARE that most define 'the eternal law' not as that law which God eternally chooses to carry out in all His works, but instead as that which He has established for all his different creatures to obey, given the different conditions in which He has created them. Those who speak this way tend to define law only as the rule of working which a superior authority imposes on another, while we on the other hand are defining it much more broadly to include any kind of rule or standard by which an action is determined. The law which they call the *eternal* law, when considered as it exists in the mind of God, has many different names when considered according to the different things it is applied to. When applied to natural agents, we call it the law of *nature*; when applied to the rule which Angels behold and obey without swerving, we call it the heavenly or *celestial* law; when applied to the law which binds reasonable creatures in such a way that they can plainly perceive it, we call it the law of *reason*; when applied to that which binds them in such a way that only special revelation can make it known, we call it the *divine* law; when applied to those laws which are derived from both reason and revelation as prudential judgments, we call it *human* law. When things are as they should be, they are conformed to this second eternal law, and even those things which do not conform to it are still ordered by the first eternal law.[1] Whatever good or evil is done under the sun, and whatever action conforms to or contradicts the law which God has imposed upon His creatures, will not God still work in it or upon it according to the law which He has chosen to keep forever (that is, the first eternal law)? Once we distinguish between these two eternal laws, it is not difficult to understand how both take place in all things.

(2.) Though we sometimes define the law of nature as the way that God has decided each created thing should act, we need to make a careful distinction. We most properly call natural agents those things which obey their laws nec-

---

[1] Hooker's distinction of a "first" and "second" eternal law is somewhat idiosyncratic and has occasioned debate among interpreters. Essentially, however, he seems here to be seeking to answer the question of why God sometimes permits things to happen, through his eternal decrees, which are at odds with his revealed will for rightly-ordered creatures. The former Hooker calls the "first eternal law," the latter the "second eternal law." Although God's will is in fact one and consistent, from our viewpoint part of it remains inscrutable, and it is to safeguard this inscrutability that Hooker distinguishes the two modes of the eternal law. The second we are given to participate in by reason (and this is what Hooker calls "the law of reason") but that does not mean we have been given to know the full mind of God, and why he does all that he does. See further, W. Bradford Littlejohn, "Cutting Through the Fog in the Channel: Hooker, Junius, and a Reformed Theology of Law," in *Richard Hooker and Reformed Orthodoxy*, ed. W. Bradford Littlejohn and Scott N. Kindred-Barnes (Göttingen: Vandenhoeck and Ruprecht, 2017), 234–39.

essarily, such as the heavens and the elements of the world, which have no choice in what they do, while we call rational beings with a free will *voluntary* agents, to set apart the two categories. In the same way, it will be helpful if we distinguish the law observed by the one from the law observed by the other—hence my category, the *law of reason*. Everyone recognizes the way that natural agents consistently keep one course, statute, and law; yet man has never achieved, nor perhaps ever will, full understanding of their ways. Perhaps God has given us so much trouble in sounding these depths, so that when we see how much more the least object in the world has within it than the wisest may comprehend, we might better learn humility.

When Moses describes the work of creation, he attributes speech to God: "Let there be light; let there be a firmament; let the waters under the firmament be gathered together into one place; let the earth bring forth; let there be lights in the firmament of the heaven." Was Moses only intending to show the greatness of God's power by how easily He did such things without travail, pain, or labor? Surely Moses had another purpose: first, to teach that God was not bound by necessity to work, but that He acted freely, intending and decreeing beforehand what outwardly proceeded from Him; second, to show that God instituted a natural law which His creatures would obey, which, according to the manner of laws, was established by solemn injunction. By commanding such things to be as they are and to keep their course as they do, He establishes the law of nature. What is the world's first creation and continued preservation but a manifestation of the eternal law of God in natural things? Just as, when once a law is published, it takes effect far and wide and everyone accommodates

THE LAW BY WHICH NATURAL AGENTS WORK

themselves to it, so also in the natural course of this world. Ever since God proclaimed the edicts of His law concerning them, heaven and earth have listened to His voice and have labored to do His will. "He made a decree for the rain" (Job 28:26), and He "placed the sand for the bound of the sea, by a perpetual decree, that it cannot pass it?" (Jer. 5:22).

If nature even for a little while were to leave off following her course and obeying her laws; if those principal and mother elements of the world from which everything in this lower world is made, were to lose their qualities; if the heavenly arch above our heads were to loosen itself and dissolve; if the celestial spheres were to forget their usual motion and by irregular turnings to go wherever they happened to go; if the prince of the lights of heaven, who like a giant runs his unwearied course, were to stand and rest as if about to faint; if the moon were to wander from her beaten path, or the times and seasons of the years to blend themselves in a disordered and confused mixture, the winds to breathe out their last gasp, the clouds to yield no rain, the earth to be bereft of all heavenly gifts, the fruits of the earth to pine away like children at the breasts of a mother who could no longer feed them; if, I say, all this were to take place, what would become of man, whom all these things serve? Do we not see plainly that <u>the obedience of all things to the law of nature is the foundation of the world?</u>

(3.) Nonetheless, the same thing often happens in nature as in art. If Phidias[2] had unyielding and obstinate stone

---

[2] Phidias was the sculptor of classical Athens, who built the statue of Zeus and statues in the Parthenon.

from which to carve, however great his skill may be, his work will lack the beauty which it might have had if it had been more pliant. Whoever strikes an instrument with skill may still make a very unpleasant sound if the string which he strikes is out of tune. Theophrastus speaks this way about the matter of natural things, saying that many things are not able to receive the best and most perfect impression.[3] The pagans who contemplated nature saw these defects in the natural world very often, but it was beyond their natural understanding to see that this was the result of God's curse due to man's sin, which he laid on creatures made for man, as God has revealed to his Church in the Gospel. But even though now and again such deviations happen in the course of nature, nevertheless, natural agents so constantly obey the laws of nature that no one denies that whatever nature does is always or for the most part consistent and uniform.[4]

(4.) If we ask what keeps nature obedient to her own law, we must remember that higher eternal law which we have already described, and since all other laws depend on it, from it we must draw whatever insight we need to resolve these questions. Not that we think, as others have, that nature acts following certain blueprints or patterns which exist in God's mind, fixing her eye on them like sailors looking to the North Star and following it. Instead, we embrace the oracle of Hippocrates that "each fulfills its allotted destiny, both unto the greater and unto the less," and that "what men work they know not, and what they

---

[3] See W.D. Ross and H.F. Forbes's translation of *Metaphysics* (Oxford: Clarendon Press, 1929), 34-35.

[4] Hooker is borrowing from Aristotle's discussion of nature in *Rhetoric* 1.39 [1369b].

THE LAW BY WHICH NATURAL AGENTS WORK

work not they think that they know; and what they see they do not understand."[5] Nonetheless, the works of nature are no less exact than if she were actually scrutinizing some shape or mirror always before her eyes. Indeed, she is so dexterous and skillful that no rational being can with all their intelligence do what she does without understanding or knowledge! Nature must have some director of infinite knowledge who guides her in all her ways. And who is the guide of nature, but the God of nature in whom we "live, and move, and have our being" (Acts 17:28)? Those things which nature is said to do are performed by divine skill with nature as the instrument. The artful workings of nature come not from any divine knowledge found in her, but only in her Guide.

Since natural things which are not voluntary agents must necessarily obey certain laws, then as long as they remain as they are, they cannot help doing what they do. Their many workings are perfectly designed for the many different purposes they achieve, but though they do what is fitting, they know neither what they do nor why they do it. From this we can see that everything they do in this way must be the result of some agent who knows, appoints, holds up, and even fashions it.

The way God does this is so far above us that we can no better imagine it with our reason than irrational creatures can understand how we arrange and determine our affairs. We only know that all things are made and ordered by the fixed purpose of divine understanding. This understanding

---

[5] Hippocrates, *Hippocrates IV: Nature of Man*, trans. W.H.S. Jones, Loeb Classical Library 150 (Cambridge, MA: Harvard University Press, 1931), 236-7 [*Regimen in Health* 1.5].

gives them their different ways of working, and we call this wisdom God's providence. The ancients called this 'natural destiny.' The law which we see carried out by natural agents is like a design in the mind of God himself, executed by the Spirit who creates and sustains every nature and natural agent as His instruments with which He works his own will and pleasure. Nature is nothing more than a tool, just as Dionysius affirmed when he saw a sudden disturbance of the world and said, "Either the God of Nature suffers, or the machine of the world is dissolved." That is, either God suffers impediment, being hindered by something greater than himself; or if that is impossible, then He must have determined to dissolve the workings of the world, since the execution of that law on which the world depends seemed to him to stand still.

This workman whose servant is nature, though only one in reality, the pagans imagined to be many: Jupiter in the sky, Juno in the air, Neptune in the water, Vesta or Ceres in the earth, Apollo in the sun, Diana in the moon, Aeolus and others in the winds, and indeed they dreamed up as many guides of nature as there were different kinds of things in the natural world. They honored these things as if they had the power to act or refrain according to what each man deserved. To us, however, there is only one Guide of all natural agents, both the Creator and Worker of all in all, alone blessed, adored, and honored by all forever and ever.

(5.) Up to this point we have been talking about natural agents taken and considered in themselves. However, we must also remember that just as each has a law which directs it to best seek its own perfection and completion, so also there is another law concerning how they must relate as parts of one body. This law binds them to serve one another's good and to prefer the good of the whole before their own particular interests, as we often see when natural agents forget their customary motions—heavy things sometimes going upward of their own accord and forsaking the earth, which is their natural resting place, just as if they had been commanded to surrender each its own private desire to fall, for the greater good of the rest of nature.

4
THE LAW BY WHICH ANGELS WORK

(1.) BUT NOW let us lift up our eyes from the footstool to the throne of God and, leaving natural things, let us consider for a space the state of heavenly and divine creatures. Angels are immaterial and rational spirits, the glorious inhabitants of the sacred palaces where there is nothing but light and blessed immortality, no cause for tears, discontentment, grief, or anxious passions, and where they dwell forever and ever, all is joy, tranquility, and peace. They are in number and order huge, mighty, and royal armies. Their obedience to the law given them by God Most High is such that when our Savior wanted to give us an idea of what we should pray and wish for on earth, He said that we should pray or wish for nothing more than that it would be with us as it is with them in heaven. God, who actively moves mere natural agents by setting them in motion, provokes rational creatures to action in a very different way, including his holy angels. Beholding the face of God, they all adore him in admiration of His great excellency, and enraptured with love, for His beauty do eternally cleave forever to Him. Their desire to resemble Him in His goodness makes them tireless and insatiable in their desire to do all the good they can to God's creatures, but especially to the children of men. Looking down on us, they see a resemblance to themselves, just as looking to God above they see what both they and men resemble. Thus far even the pagans have approached, so that Orpheus confesses that "before thy burning throne the angels wait, much-working, charged to do all things for men,"[1] and that mirror of human wisdom, Aristotle, has said that God moves angels to act in the same way as good and beautiful things stir the heart of man to action.[2] Angels may therefore act in three ways: first with most wonderful love rising from the sight of the purity, glory and beauty of the God who is visible only to spirits that are pure; second with adoration grounded on the proof of the greatness of God, on whom they see all other things depend; third with imitation, nourished by the presence of the perfect goodness of Him who never ceases to fill heaven and earth with the treasures of his free and undeserved grace.

(2.) We must not only consider what angels are and do individually, but also what concerns them as they are linked into a single body among themselves and have fellowship with men. Considering angels individually, their law is that which the prophet David says, "Praise ye Him, all His angels" (Ps. 148:2). Considering them corporately,

---

[1] Quoted by Clement of Alexandria, *Miscellanies* 5.14, in *Ante-Nicene Fathers of the Church*, vol. 2, *Fathers of the Second Century: Hermas, Tatian, Athenagoras, Theophilus, and Clement of Alexandria*, ed. Alexander Roberts and James Donaldson (1885; Peabody, MA: Hendrickson Publishers, 1994), 473.

[2] Aristotle, *Metaphysics* 12.7 [1072a].

their law makes them an army, some in rank and degree above others. Considering them, lastly, as having that communion with us which the author of Hebrews recognizes (12:22) and calls them our fellow-servants (Rev. 22:9), from this we see a third law, which binds them to the work of ministering. All these tasks they do with joy.

(3.) Nonetheless, some of these angels have fallen and their fall has come through the voluntary breach of that law which demanded that they continue to exercise their high and admirable virtue. They never could have changed or desired to omit any part of their duty unless something had been able to turn their hearts from God, and drawn them astray before they attained that high perfection of bliss which now prevents the elect angels from falling. They could never have preferred anything to God as long as they saw that it depended upon God, since God would have seemed infinitely better than anything else they would have seen. Anything beneath them was so obviously dependent on God that they could not see it otherwise, so the only way they could sin was by turning to reflect on themselves and their own sublimity, thus forgetting their subordination to God. Their dependence on Him was drowned in this fantasy, and so their adoration, love, and imitation of God were interrupted. The fall of angels therefore was pride. Since their fall, they have been doing the exact opposite of the duties just described. They were dispersed, some in the air, some on the earth, some under the water, some among the minerals, dens, and caves under the earth, but by all means they desire to bring about universal disobedience to the laws of God and as much as they can to destroy His works. The pagans honored these wicked spirits as gods, calling them "infernal gods" and seeing them in oracles, idols, household gods, and nymphs. There was no foul or wicked spirit which men did not somehow honor as God until the light appeared in the world and dissolved the works of the devil. This suffices for a description of angels; the next in order are *men*.

5
THE LAW BY WHICH MAN IS DIRECTED TO THE IMITATION OF GOD

(1.) WITH THE exception of God who absolutely and eternally is who He is, all other things have some susceptibility to change and to become that which they are not now. This is why all things have desire, which makes them incline to change into what they may become, and once they have changed, they are more perfect than they were. Such perfections we call *goodness*. And since anything in the world might serve to make another thing better than it is, all things that exist are good.

(2.) Again, since all goodness proceeds from God, the supreme cause of all things, and since every effect in its fashion resembles its cause, all things in the world are said to somehow seek the highest and to desire, some more, some less, participation in God Himself.[1] However, nothing in the universe displays this as much as man, because

---

[1] Aristotle, *On the Soul* 2.4 [415ab].

THE LAW BY WHICH MAN IS DIRECTED TO IMITATE GOD

man seeks so many different kinds of perfection. The most fundamental sort of goodness, which all things seek, is their continued existence. Therefore since everything desires to be like God in His immortality, those things which cannot achieve it for themselves individually, seek to perpetuate themselves through their offspring. The second level of goodness by which things seek to resemble God is by constantly and excellently doing whatever it is that their kind does. They strive after God's immutability by working always or for the most part in the same manner; they imitate his absolute exactness by tending toward an exquisite excellence of form. From this come the axioms of philosophy showing how nature's works cannot be bettered.[2]

(3.) These two kinds of goodness are so integral to those which desire them that we are scarcely aware of ourselves desiring them. However, the desire for further goods external to us is more obvious, especially those which must be known before they can be consciously desired, or which are desired for the mere sake of knowing them. Concerning such goods, man, uniquely among the creatures of this world, aspires to the greatest conformity with God by pursuing the knowledge of truth and by growing in the exercise of virtue. We Christians, who have been instructed by God, are not the only ones aware of this unique calling, but those who are further from God also acknowledge this. What did Plato do more often than excite men to love wisdom by showing them how much it exalted wise men above other men, and made them, though not gods, yet like gods, high, admirable, and divine? Similarly, Hermes Trismegistus, speaking of the vir-

---

[2] Aristotle, *On the Heavens* 2.5 [288a].

tues of the righteous soul, says that these spirits never busy themselves with the praise of men, but with performing good in word and deed, because it is their office to conform themselves to the pattern of the Father of spirits.[3]

---

[3] Hermes Trismegistus, *The Key* 21. Cf. *The Corpus Hermeticum*, trans. G. Mead (United States of America: IAP, 2009), 29, which translates it "such a soul doth never tire in songs of praise [to God] and pouring blessing on all men, and doing good in word and deed to all, in imitation of its Sire."

6
HOW MEN FIRST BEGIN TO KNOW THE LAW THEY SHOULD OBSERVE

(1.) IN THE matter of knowledge, there is a difference between angels and men: angels already have full and complete knowledge to the highest degree possible for them, whereas men are at birth without any understanding or knowledge at all. Nonetheless, from this complete ignorance they grow little by little until they come to be just as the angels are. What the one has now, the other shall reach at the last, and they are not so far apart that they will never meet someday. The soul of man at first is like a book in which nothing is written, but in which anything might be. We will now consider the steps by which our knowledge grows to perfection.

(2.) To our discussion of natural agents above, we must add that, although we have included both living and nonliving things, whatever is lower in nature than man, if we are to be more precise we must distinguish between natural agents that work completely unconsciously and those agents that have some notion, though weak, of what they are doing, such as fishes, birds, and beasts. Beasts have senses just as sharp as ours, and sometimes even more so. (Notice how stones, though lesser than plants in dignity, surpass them in their firmness and durability, and in the same way plants, though less in excellency than creatures with sense-experience, far outdo them in their growth and fertility; just so beasts, though in other ways less than men, may yet be beyond them in senses and instinct. A creature which seeks some high perfection is often more lacking when it comes to some lower perfection, since it is not as important to it as to a creature which has nothing higher to seek.)

(3.) Since the soul of man is capable of a more divine perfection, he has besides his growth in sense experience the further ability to reach higher than sensible things, an ability which beasts do not possess at all. Until we reach a certain age, our souls only fill themselves with ideas that are lesser and easier to understand, which later on serve as a means to greater understanding, but for the moment are not any higher than those of beasts. Once they comprehend anything beyond this, such as differences of time, affirmations, negations, and contradictions, then we say that they have come to use natural reason. If afterwards we add proper instruction in true art and learning, there would be just as much a difference of understanding between such men and those we see around us as between men and infants (not that our own age, for all its pretensions of learning, knows or cares much about such instruction). If you think I am exaggerating, consider this: no discipline is at its first discovery so perfect as it is once men have cultivated it, yet the first man, who took any trouble to follow the method we have described, Aristotle, achieved more in almost every branch of natural knowledge than anyone else has ever done in any single branch.

(4.) (Even though the newly devised method of Peter Ramus[1] is rather lacking, there are two things about it which stand out. It is very quick and teaches its practitioners as much in three days as in thirty years. Again, since man's curiosity may sometimes carry him away more deeply into certain questions than is wise, this method limits him to such general topics that are so basic that even the most slow-witted of men may understand them. Following its rules and precepts, we may define it as a method that teaches speedy discourse and keeps men's minds from getting too wise.)

(5.) By education and instruction, that is, forming habits and teaching principles, we make our faculty of reason more apt to judge rightly between truth and error, good and evil. But common sense, not skill or learning, can best perceive at what age a man has attained to such use of reason to discern those laws which guide his actions, just as the blacksmith knows better how much to heat his fire than any natural philosopher does.

---

[1] Peter Ramus (1515–72) was a French Reformed humanist and logician who was known for his hostility against the Aristotelian logic and pedagogical method that had dominated European scholarship for many centuries. Such anti-Aristotelianism was not uncommon among 16th-century humanists, but Ramus was the first to offer a plausible alternative method, which was meant to be much simpler, and relied heavily on binary divisions. Although initially influential and preferred especially by some Calvinist theologians for elucidating doctrinal problems, Hooker's disdainful assessment here was to prove in time well-judged. For further reading, see Walter J. Ong, *Ramus, Method, and the Decay of Dialogue: From the Art of Discourse to the Art of Reason* (Cambridge, MA: Harvard University Press, 1958).

7
MAN'S WILL, WHICH LAWS OF ACTION ARE MADE TO GUIDE

(1.) BY REASON, man knows both things that are discovered by the senses and those that are not. We must then ask how man comes to know those non-sensible things that must be known for the sake of action. Since nothing can move without being drawn to an end, how can that divine power of the soul, that "spirit of our mind" as the Apostle calls it (Eph. 4:23), ever rouse itself to action, unless it also has such a spur? Sometimes we are moved to an action which we consider good for its own sake. (Indeed, some turbulent minds think disturbing the status quo reason enough to act![1]) Sometimes, though, we act for the sake of some other good we hope to achieve, such as those whom our Savior described as giving alms to purchase the praise of men.

---

[1] Sallust's *Catiline War* 1.21. See William W. Batstone, *Catiline's Conspiracy, The Jugurthine War, Histories* (Oxford: OUP, 2010), 21, which similarly translates it as "they thought that the disruption of the status quo was a great reward in itself."

(2.) Man in his perfection has been made in the likeness of His maker and he resembles Him also in how he acts. Whatever we do as men, we do freely and consciously, and unlike natural agents we have the power of leaving any action undone. The goods which provoke us to action cannot do so unless we first apprehend them as good and so desire them, and once we see them as good, we cannot help but prefer doing them over not doing them. Choice, however, means that whatever we do, we also could have left undone. If fire consumes stubble, it cannot help it, because that is its nature. To choose is to will one thing instead of another, and to will is to bend ourselves to having or doing something which we deem good. Goodness is seen with the eye of the understanding, and the light of that eye is reason. The two fountains of human action are knowledge and will, and when the will tends towards a particular end, we call it choice. Concerning knowledge, Moses has said, "See, I have set before thee this day life and good, and death and evil," and concerning the will he adds, "choose life" (Dt. 30:15, 19), which means that we must choose those things that lead to life.

(3.) But we must pay special attention to how the will is, strictly speaking, very different from that lesser desire which we call the appetite. Appetite seeks whatever goods are perceived by the senses and then wished for, while the will seeks whatever good reason points out. Passions such as joy, grief, fear, anger, and so forth are different aspects of the appetite, which will not rise at the sight of something indifferent, but cannot help rising at the sight of certain things. Therefore, it is not entirely within our power to choose whether we will be aroused by passions or not, while actions springing from our will *are* within our power to do or not to do. Appetite coaxes the will, and will controls the appetite, and what one desires, the other often rejects. The will, properly speaking, comes into play whenever reason and understanding tell us (or at least appear to tell us) what to desire.

Some may ask, then, whether men's actions are voluntary, when goods perceived with our senses awaken the appetite so that we take action, without reason ever entering into the equation, such as when we eat, drink, rest, and so on. The fact is that such actions (in those who have the use of reason) are voluntary. Consider how a ruler's authority extends even to those things that are too trivial for his subordinates to consult him about; just so, we are said to act voluntarily in cases when the will could have vetoed some action, though our reason does not bother to consider it. In such cases, the will gives assent by silence, and is less noticeable than in cases when the will expressly commands or prohibits, and especially when we need to consult with ourselves before proceeding.

(4.) When understanding is required, reason is said to direct man's will by considering what action is best, and the commands of right reason generate the principles of right behavior. Children do not have the full use of right reason yet, the mentally defective by their nature cannot have it at all, and madmen have temporarily lost the use of it; thus all these need to be guided by the reason of those who seek what is best for them. Among the rest is the light of reason, which distinguishes good from evil and when it does this correctly, it is called right reason.

(5.) Nonetheless, the will does not follow reason's commands, unless reason shows that such things are possible.

MAN'S WILL

Though appetite can desire anything that seems good, a reasonable will never pursues anything that is impossible. If reason judges something impossible, the will lets it go.

(6.) Man's will has the natural freedom to take or refuse anything put before it, and whatever good it may seek might always be accompanied by something difficult or unpleasant, which might make the will shrink back and give up. On the other hand, whatever is evil may yet have an appearance of goodness, drawing us after it. For nothing evil is desired as such, and is only chosen because of a goodness which is or at least seems to be attached to it. Likewise, it is not the *existence* of goodness, but the *appearance* of it that provokes us to action; therefore many precious things are neglected, simply because their true worth is hidden. Goodness perceived by the senses is apparent, near, and present, and as such it arouses our appetite. In short, the will acts in pursuit of whatever good that the understanding perceives, grounded on the senses (or refuses to act in the absence of any perceived good)—unless, that is, some higher reason overrules it. And whenever our reason judges rightly that something is good, still, so long as there is any uncertainty, there is room for the will to choose otherwise. Since there are so many duties to be done, and so few where the reason can easily and certainly discover the right course, it is no surprise when men choose evil, even when the contrary is knowable. This is how habit often wins out over reason, accustoming us to act as we always have, without pausing to think. Reason may therefore discern the good, and yet the will refuse it, as long as we are slaves to our sense experience.

(7.) However, this does not give any man a legitimate excuse for sin. For no sin has ever been committed without some lesser good being willfully preferred to a greater good, which would disgrace our nature and overturn the divine order that commands us to always choose the highest good. Every good that concerns us is evident enough that, if we diligently consider it by reason, we cannot fail to recognize it. When we neglect to use our reason, we are easily led astray by fantasies: sometimes when deceived by Satan's wiles, as Eve was; sometimes when through hastiness we do not use our reason at all, such as when the Apostles, seeing something that displeased them, immediately asked for fire from heaven; sometimes when the habit of evildoing has hardened our hearts against any instruction, as with those over whom our Savior wept and said, "O Jerusalem, how often and you would not!" Nevertheless, we cannot excuse ourselves when we do evil, preferring a lesser good over a greater good, when the latter's superiority could be discovered by reason. Seeking knowledge is rather painful, and this is why the will is often so reluctant to pursue it. This is the result of the Curse, by which our souls' faculties of reason have been so weakened that they prefer to rest in ignorance rather than taking the trouble to find out the truth. We need some incentive to seek out the truth, which is why we have a natural thirst for knowledge planted within us. But that original weakness in our faculties, which afflicts our every attempt to reason, makes us hesitate at the slightest sign of toil. This is why the Apostle, knowing that the weariness of the flesh so often stands in the way of the will, harps on this theme: "Awake thou that sleepest"; "lay aside every weight," "watch ye," "seek," "strive to enter in by the narrow door" (Eph. 5:14; Heb. 12:1; 1 Cor. 16:13; Prov. 2:4; Luke 13:24).

8
OF THE NATURAL WAY TO FIND OUT LAWS BY REASON TO LEAD THE WILL TO WHAT IS GOOD

(1) LET US return to our earlier plan of exploring the natural way by which we discover the rules of goodness that guide man's will in all his actions. Just as everything naturally and necessarily desires the highest perfection it is capable of achieving, so does man. Since our happiness is the object of all our desires, we cannot help but wish it. Whatever falls within the scope of human action, the will inclines to it to the extent that our reason judges it better for us, and ultimately better for our happiness. If reason errs, we fall into evil and are deprived of the general perfection we seek. Since knowledge of good and evil is so necessary for right action, all that is left is to ask how we might possess it. We should not suppose that there is one way of recognizing good and another of recognizing evil. For whoever knows what is straight likewise knows what is crooked, since crookedness is just the absence of straight-

ness in bodies that are capable of it.[1] Goodness in actions is the same way, and what we do well we call "right." Just as the straight way is the best way for a traveler to reach his destination soonest, so the action that best leads us to our desire is the most fitting. Not only that, but in straightness we find beauty, and in crookedness, ugliness; whatever is good in men's actions is not only profitable, but also beautiful. (It is interesting to note in this regard that the Greeks used the same word—*kalos*—to refer to both beauty and goodness in human action,[2] whereas our word "good" generally only refers to the latter. But here, I am using it to imply both.)

(2.) There are only two ways to recognize goodness: knowing the causes that make something good, or looking at the signs and marks which always accompany things that are good, even if we cannot see right away why they are good in and of themselves. The first way is the best method, but it is so difficult that everyone avoids it and would rather walk aimlessly as if in the dark than tread such long and intricate mazes for the sake of knowledge. Just as physicians often must forego the best remedies, and prescribe treatments that their impatient patients will accept, just so in this present age, so full of tongue and weak of brain, we should defer to the majority. We do not make any deep inquiry about the causes of goodness, save touching on them here and there when they are particularly close at hand. We choose instead that way of proving things, which, though inferior in itself, is better suited to the feeblemindedness of our days.

---

[1] Aristotle *On the Soul* 1.5 [411a].

[2] Aristotle, *Magna Moralia* 2.9 [1207b]; *Politics* 4.6 [1293b].

THE NATURAL WAY TO FIND OUT LAWS BY REASON

(3.) There are many signs and marks by which we can recognize goodness, some more certain and some less. The most certain mark of goodness is the general conviction of all humanity. Therefore a commonly-held falsehood is not refuted until we go from signs to causes, demonstrating that there is a common confusion at the root of the error that explains why so many men have been led astray. In such a case, surmisings and probabilities are not enough to refute it, since the universal agreement of men is the best of these kinds of proofs that we can offer. Times change, and what one man happens to think will not often be thought so forever. Therefore, although we may not yet see why, we know there has to be some necessary reason when nearly all men at nearly all times agree on something, especially on matters of natural philosophy. It is agreed that things acting according to their nature all keep to the same course.[3] The general and perpetual voice of mankind is as the judgment of God Himself, since what all men at all times have come to believe must have been taught to them by Nature, and since God is Nature's author, her voice is merely His instrument. There are any number of duties we must perform that are made clear enough by this rule alone, without any further warrant being needed. The Apostle Paul says that the pagans are a "law to themselves" (Rom. 2:14), meaning that God illuminates all men with the light of reason so that they can know truth from falsehood and good from evil. By reasoning together they learn what the will of God is, without any supernatural revelation, and thus, when they seem to be making their own laws, they are in fact merely discovering His.

---

[3] Aristotle *Rhetoric* 1.39 [1369b].

(4.) Therefore, we may define a law in general as a rule that directs something how to act well. The rule for divine activity in time and history is determined by God's wisdom found within Himself. The rule for natural agents that act without free will is also determined by God's wisdom, and is known to God, but not to them. The rule for natural agents, such as beasts, who work consciously after their own fashion, is an instinct based on their senses about what is good for them. The rule for immaterial natures, such as spirits and angels, is an immediate intuition and recognition of the beauty and high goodness of God, their end, which makes them work with unspeakable joy and delight. The rule for voluntary agents on earth is the judgment of reason about what things are the best to be done. And reason teaches us first of general principles before it speaks to particular situations.

(5.) The main principles taught by reason are obvious in and of themselves. After all, if nothing were self-evident we would not know anything; as Theophrastus says, those who seek for a reason for all things utterly overthrow all reason.[4] In every subject, there are some basic propositions that, once they have been mentioned, we cannot help seeing that they are undeniably true, even without proof. An example of such an axiom is "the greater good should be preferred to the lesser good." Our natural tendency is to avoid the painful and seek the pleasant. If we ask why we should ignore this tendency, and instead despise the pleasures of sin and rejoice in the struggles of virtue, we never would unless wisdom clearly told us that great goods are

---

[4] See W.D. Ross and H.F. Forbes's translation of *Metaphysics* (Oxford: Clarendon Press, 1929), 28-29.

THE NATURAL WAY TO FIND OUT LAWS BY REASON

worth small difficulties, whereas fleeting pleasures are not worth the unspeakable harms that follow them. This is the ground of Paul's exhortation to patience: "For our light affliction, which is for the moment, worketh for us more and more exceedingly an eternal weight of glory; while we look not at the things which are seen, but at the things which are not seen: for the things which are seen are temporal; but the things which are not seen are eternal" (2 Cor. 4:17-18). This is why Christianity was to be embraced, despite all the hardships accompanying it at the time. For the same reason, our Savior shows how futile it is to sin for gain: "For what shall a man be profited, if he shall gain the whole world, and forfeit his life? Or what shall a man give in exchange for his life?" (Mt. 16:26). More specific axioms that still need no further proof are these: God should be worshiped, parents should be honored, we should treat others as we wish to be treated, etc. Such things, once said, compel our agreement, and require no further proof or discussion to convince us of their truth.

Nonetheless, any such axiom was first discovered by rational discourse and drawn from out of the very bowels of heaven and earth. For we must note that we seek knowledge of the world not merely so far as is useful for survival, but also for two other higher reasons: first, even if there were no other use, our minds are by nature so delighted with understanding that we would seek such knowledge purely for its own sake; second, the understanding of nature gives us rules, principles, and laws by which human actions can be properly directed. This is why the pagans made the goddess Themis, called by us Justice or Right, the daughter of Heaven and Earth.

(6.) Again, we know things either as they are in themselves or as they are in relation to one another. Knowledge of both what man is in himself and what he is in relation to all other things is the mother of all the edicts, statutes, and decrees in the law of nature, by which human actions are guided. When the best things rule, the best things follow. Thus, when we see how much worthier our souls are than our bodies, and the more divine part of our souls than the baser part, it is clear that all is not well unless the greater commands and directs the lesser. The soul should direct the body, and the spirit of our minds, the soul. This is the first law: that in every action, the highest power of the mind demands the obedience of the other faculties of our nature.

(7.) There are several other chief commands imposed by the mind to be obeyed by the will, and they are found by the same method, whether they have to do with duties toward God or man.

Concerning God, I do not have the time to explain how, little by little, men come to know, by nature alone, not only that there is a God, but also what power, force, and wisdom He has and how everything depends on Him. This being granted, then, men have recognized our relationship to God as his children,[5] and the fact that all good things depend on him as their First Cause,[6] and thus have arrived at such laws as 'in all things we go about, his aid is to be

---

[5] Plato, *Theaetetus* [151D]. Jowett translates the original as "no god is the enemy of man."

[6] Aristotle, *Metaphysics* 1.2 [983a]. Joe Sachs translates this as "for the divine seems to be among the causes for all things, and to be a certain sources." *Metaphysics* (Santa Fe, NM: Green Lion Press, 1999), 5.

craved'[7] and 'He cannot have sufficient honor done unto Him, but the utmost of that we can do to honor Him we must do'.[8] This is just another way of saying, "You shall love the Lord your God with all your heart, with all your soul, and with all your strength," (Dt. 6:5) which our Savior calls the first and greatest commandment (Matt. 22:38).

As for the other command, which our Savior says is like it, it is the root from which we derive all laws concerning our duties to our fellow man, and here too, men have naturally tended to see that it is their duty to love others just as much as themselves. For, since things that are equal must be treated equally, how can I expect good from another unless I am willing to offer him the same satisfaction of his desires, seeing as we all share the same nature? They would be as upset to be mistreated as I would be, and if I do harm, I must not be surprised when I suffer, since others have little reason to show any greater love to me than I have showed to them. If I desire to be loved by my fellow man as much as possible, I have a duty to show him the same affection that I hope to receive. From this basic human equality, our natural reason deduces several laws by which to direct our lives, of which no man is ignorant, such as: since we wish not to be harmed, we must not harm others, and since we do not wish to be dealt with harshly, we must not deal with others harshly, and we must

---

[7] Plato *Timaeus* [27C]. Jowett translates the original thus: "All men, Socrates, who have any degree of right feeling, at the beginning of every enterprise, whether small or great, always call upon God."

[8] Aristotle, *Nicomachean Ethics* 8 [1163b]. Again, Sachs: "no one could ever give back what they deserve, and one who does them honor as far as possible seems to be a decent person." *Aristotle's Nicomachean Ethics* (Newburyport, MA: Focus Publishing, 2002), 162.

abstain from all violence and wrong, and so on.[9] It would be pointless to elaborate, and unnecessary for our purposes, since all particular prescriptions follow from these two principles.

(8.) Therefore, the natural way to determine how we should act is the judgment of reason, setting down what is good to do. This judgment is either mandatory, showing what *must* be done; or else permissive, declaring only what *may* be done; or else advisory, revealing what is *most prudent* for us to do. A mandatory judgment always confronts us with a choice between doing and not doing something in itself absolutely good or evil, as in the case of Joseph, who had to choose whether or not to yield to his mistress's lust. A permissive judgment is when, faced with multiple bad choices, which we cannot avoid, we are allowed to choose an option that would not otherwise be permitted, as in the case of divorce among the Jews. An advisory judgment is when, faced with multiple good choices, one is better than the rest, as with the first Christians who sold their possessions and laid the money at the feet of the Apostles, even though they might have kept their possessions without sinning. Another example of this is when St. Paul chose to support himself by his own work, even though he might have lived off of the church's support without sinning. For there are gradations in goodness, such that even among good actions, some are better than others. After all, if all good actions were equal, no one good man could be better

---

[9] These quotes are all taken from the laws of Justinian. See *Codex*, ed. Paul Krueger, in *Corpus Juris Civilis*, (Berlin: Weidmanns, 1884-1963), Headnote to Justinian 3.28.11; *Digest*, ed. Theodore Mommsen, in *Corpus Juris Civilis* (Berlin: Weidmanns, 1884-1963), 47, 745 [2.2; 43.24.1].

THE NATURAL WAY TO FIND OUT LAWS BY REASON

than another good man, but everyone would be completely good or not at all—as if goodness were some single point on a target which you either hit or missed completely. In that case, goodness could vary only by how often or seldom one practiced it. However, since goodness is broader than that, a law properly speaking is something which reason says *must* be done. And the law of reason or human nature is that which men have discovered, by process of natural reasoning, that they are perpetually and universally bound by.

(9.) We know the laws of reason by these marks, and those who keep them resemble in their actions the works of nature herself. All of nature's works are necessary, and beautiful, with nothing superfluous or lacking, and so will be the works of anyone who follows the law of reason. These laws can be discovered through reason, even without divine revelation, and indeed are so apparent upon investigation that they have been known to the world from the beginning of time. As Sophocles says of one branch of the law, "It is alive, not just of today or yesterday, it lives forever, from the first of time, and no one knows when it first saw the light."[10] It has not merely been affirmed by one or two or few, but by all men. This does not mean that every single individual in the world knows and acknowledges the entire law of reason, but that, once the law of reason is described, no one can reject it as unreasonable or unjust. There is nothing in it that any man with the full use of his wits and in possession of sound judgment will not

---

[10] Sophocles, *Antigone*, trans. Robert Fagles, in *The Theban Cycle* (New York: Penguin, 1984), 82 [lines 506-508]. The wording has been altered from plural to match Hooker's quotation.

find out if he searches diligently enough. Finally, it is difficult to find men who are ignorant of the general principles of the laws of reason. Men often call these laws, "the law of nature," because this is the law which human nature is universally obligated by reason to follow, but our term "the law of reason" seems more precise. This law encompasses everything which men naturally know (or at least may naturally know) to be seemly or unseemly, virtuous or vicious, good or evil.

(10.) Now, the saying is true that 'every wrong action violates the law of nature and reason.'[11] For, although transgressions against supernatural laws do not violate the law of reason *as such*, they do inasmuch as they are evil and thus violate the principle that we must always flee from evil. However, we do not want to define the law of reason so broadly that it includes all the laws which we as creatures are obligated to obey, but we restrict it to those which all men with their natural understanding might recognize as their duties. Saint Augustine notes that some

> aroused by this diversity of innumerable customs, some souls, drowsy so to speak, who were neither settled in the sound sleep of folly nor able to waken fully to the light of wisdom, have thought that justice did not exist of itself, but that each nation regarded as right that which was its own custom. Since this or that custom is different for every nation, while justice must remain immutable, it becomes evident that there is no justice anywhere. They have not understood (not to

---

[11] Cf. Aquinas, *Summa Theologica* I-II, q. 94, art. 3; and Augustine, *City of God* 12.1.

> multiply instances) that the maxim, 'Do not do to another what you do not wish to have done to you,' cannot be varied in any way by any national diversity of customs. When this rule is applied to the love of God, all vices die; when it is applied to the love of our neighbor, all crimes vanish.[12]

Therefore, Saint Augustine's opinion concerning the law of reason seems to be that it includes universally agreed-upon principles, and from these self-evident principles, we can discover our greatest moral duties to God or man with little difficulty.

(11.) Some may object that, if the greatest part of the moral law is so easily known, why then are so many people ignorant of even basic moral duties, such that it does not even occur to them that they are sinning? I do not deny that perverted and wicked customs—perhaps beginning with a few and spreading to the multitude, and then continuing for a long time—may be so strong that they smother the light of our natural understanding, because men refuse to make an effort to consider whether their customs are good or evil. An example of this would be pagan worship of idols, the works of their own hands, which was so palpably absurd that the Prophet David compared idolaters to idols as equally lacking in sense and intelligence: "They that make them shall be like unto them; yea, every one that trusteth in them" (Ps. 135:18). The wise man says of the foolishness of the idolater that

---

[12] Augustine, *On Christian Instruction*, trans. John S. Gavigan, in *The Fathers of the Church: The Writings of Saint Augustine*, vol. 4, ed. Roy Joseph Deferrari (New York: Fathers of the Church, 1945), 134-135 [3.14].

when he prays about possessions and his marriage and children, he is not ashamed to address a lifeless thing. For health he appeals to a thing that is weak; for life he prays to a thing that is dead; for aid he entreats a thing that is utterly inexperienced; for a prosperous journey, a thing that cannot take a step; for money-making and work and success with his hands he asks strength of a thing whose hands have no strength. (Wisd. 13:17)

Later on he attributes this stupidity to custom:

> For a father, consumed with grief at an untimely bereavement, made an image of his child, who had been suddenly taken from him; and he now honored as a god what was once a dead human being, and handed on to his dependents secret rites and initiations. Then the ungodly custom, grown strong with time, was kept as a law, and at the command of monarchs graven images were worshiped. (Wisd. 14:15-16)[13]

The authority of rulers, the ambition of craftsmen, and the like thus propelled the ignorant and increased their superstition.

More may be added to what this wise man has said. Whatever I have said or will say about man's natural understanding, I want this to be clear: no faculty or power of either man or any creature can rightly perform any of its allotted functions without the perpetual aid and concurrence of Him that causes all things. Once God withdraws

---

[13] All quotations from the Apocrypha are taken from the Revised Standard Version (RSV).

THE NATURAL WAY TO FIND OUT LAWS BY REASON

His support, the only possible result, as the Apostle says, is that men who have been blessed with the light of reason will walk "in the vanity of their mind, being darkened in their understanding, alienated from the life of God, because of the ignorance that is in them, because of the hardening of their heart" (Eph. 4:17-18). This cause is also described by the Prophet Isaiah who speaks of the ignorance of idolaters who cannot see how the Law of Reason manifestly condemns their wickedness and sin: "neither is there knowledge nor understanding to say, 'shall I fall down to the stock of a tree?' They know not, neither do they consider: for he hath shut their eyes, that they cannot see" (Is. 44:19, 18).

What we have just said about idolatry equally applies to any instance where a great blindness has prevailed against the manifest laws of reason. Among these laws we include not only those which may easily be known to be all men's duty, but also whatever of the same sort that can possibly be discovered by good and necessary consequence. For if we begin talking about probabilities about what is most convenient for men to do, we will have passed into the territory of free and discretionary decisions, where human laws are made, which we will consider later.

9
THE ADVANTAGES OF KEEPING THE LAW TAUGHT BY REASON

(1.) THE LAWS taught by reason are of no small benefit to those that keep them. For we see that the world is so knit together that when each part of it performs only its natural function, it preserves both itself and everything around it. If the sun or the moon or any of the heavenly bodies were to cease or fail or swerve from their natural course, would not the immediate result be the their ruin and the ruin of everything that depended on them? And since man is not only the noblest creature in the world, but also a world within himself, is it not clear that by transgressing the law of his nature he would bring great harm upon the earth? Yes, "tribulation and anguish, upon every soul of man that worketh evil" (Rom. 2:9).

Good always results when things observe the course of their nature, and evil results when they do the opposite, but in the case of natural agents, we do not properly call this "reward" or "punishment." This is because among all the creatures found in the world, only man's keeping of

THE ADVANTAGES OF KEEPING THE LAW OF REASON

the law is *righteousness*, and his transgression alone is *sin*. For when man obeys or disobeys the law of his nature, he always chooses voluntarily. Anything we do against our will, or under compulsion, we are not truly said to do, since what makes us do it is not inside us, but outside us, driving us along as the wind blows a feather in the air. In such cases, the evil done by the unwilling makes us compassionate. Such men are pitied and thought to be miserable rather than culpable.

Furthermore, sometimes men do things, though not outwardly constrained, still without their wills, such as when they lose their minds or otherwise wholly lack capacity for judgment. This is why no one sees fit to punish the actions of madmen or the mentally defective. And we do some things neither against our wills, nor completely with them, but sometimes our wills are moved in such a way that although it is possible to act differently it is not easy. This is why we consider certain evil deeds to be more pardonable than others. Finally, our evil deeds are more excusable to the degree that the situation constrains us, unless this arises through our own fault. So, for instance, a drunk man who commits incest and complains that he was out of his mind hardly has a good excuse: it was up to him to decide whether to get out of his mind in the first place. Rewards and punishments always presuppose something good or bad done willingly; good and bad things may happen to us regardless of what we have done, but in such cases we call them advantages and hurts, not rewards or punishments. From these various dispositions of the will, the source of all men's actions, come the many rewards and punishments which are determined by such rules as these: "Take away the will, and all acts are equal: that which we do not, and would do, is commonly accepted as done."[1] By these standards do we conclude whether men's actions should be rewarded or punished.

(2.) Rewards and punishments are only given by those above us capable of examining and judging our deeds. We will carefully consider later on how men come to have this authority over one another, as far as public actions are concerned, but for now everyone admits that every man's heart and conscience approves or condemns his own actions, even those done in secret, and either rejoices and hopes for reward or grieves and fears future punishment. The only one from whom we may expect such reward and punishment is He who discerns and judges the secrets of all hearts; for He alone rewards and avenges all such secret actions, and not only those done in secret, but also all violations against His law of nature. This is why the Roman "Laws of the Twelve Tables," when they require such inward affections which the eye of man cannot perceive, threaten men who neglect to obey with divine punishment.[2]

---

[1] Justinian, *Codex*, ed. Paul Krueger, in *Corpus Juris Civilis*, (Berlin: Weidmanns, 1884-1963), lex foedissimam and lex si quis in testamen. We have retained Hooker's own translation here.

[2] See Cicero, *De Legibus*, 2.19, 24. See *The Republic and the Laws*, trans. Niall Rudd (Oxford: OUP, 1998), 128, 131.

10
HOW REASON LEADS MEN TO MAKE THE LAWS BY WHICH POLITICAL SOCIETIES ARE GOVERNED, AND TO AGREE ABOUT LAWS OF FELLOWSHIP BETWEEN INDEPENDENT SOCIETIES

(1.) WHAT WE have said up to this point is, I hope, enough to show how foolish those men are who imagine that religion and virtue are only what men make them to be, as if they were not rooted in nature and could be totally otherwise if customs were different. On the contrary, nature itself teaches us the laws and statutes by which we must live. The laws which we have discussed thus far obligate all men, by virtue of their humanity, to obey them, even if they never form any social ties or solemnly agree about what to do or not to do.

However, as solitary individuals we cannot provide ourselves with all the things that we need to make a life fit for the dignity of man. Therefore, we naturally seek communion and fellowship with others to supply whatever we lack as individuals. This is why men first banded together and formed political societies. Such societies need governments, and governments need a kind of law distinct from that which we have been discussing. There are two pillars which uphold public societies: first, a natural inclination towards sociable life and fellowship, and second, some arrangement, whether implicit or explicit, governing the order of their common life together. This agreement is what we call the Law of a Commonweal and it is the soul of every political body, animated by laws which set it to work for the sake of the common good. Political laws, established for the sake of public order, are never properly devised unless they presume that man's will is obstinate, rebellious, and completely opposed to obeying the sacred laws of his nature. In other words, laws are not sound unless they assume that man in his depravity is little better than a beast, and they moderate his actions to prevent any hindrance to the common good. It remains therefore to consider how we can discover laws which serve to direct even depraved natures towards a right end.

(2.) All men desire to lead a happy life in this world. The most happy life is that in which we exercise our virtue without impediment. The Apostle exhorts men to be content in this world even if they have nothing more than food and clothing, which would imply that these are the bare minimum of what is necessary for life. If we were stripped of all else, we would at least need these, and if we are without them, we will not care about anything else. This is why God first told Adam to sustain himself and then gave him a law to obey (Gen. 1:29; 2:17), and this is also why the first thing we read of, after we learn that men began to increase, is that they engaged in the tilling of earth and the feeding of cattle. Only after their sustenance is secured, do we read of their religious practices (Gen. 4:2, 26). While it is true that the kingdom of God must be first in our hearts and our desires, a righteous life presupposes life, and we cannot live virtuously unless we first live. Therefore the first need we seek to satisfy is the need for our bare necessities. Many tools are necessary for life, and many more if, like most men, we seek a life with joy, comfort, delight, and pleasure. This is why so many different arts and inventions were so quickly discovered at the very beginning of the world (Gen. 4:20-22).

Just as things of necessity are always provided for first, so also things of greatest dignity are most regarded by those who judge rightly. Although all men may wish for riches, yet no one with sense can imagine that it is better to be rich than to be wise, virtuous, and godly. If we are rich or wise or both this is not because we are born that way. We enter the world with neither, as naked in mind as in body. Man begins dependent upon the household, just as the Prophet says, "Can a woman forget her sucking child?" (Is. 49:15). This is what the Apostle has in mind when he says that "if any provideth not for his own, and specially his own household, he hath denied the faith, and is worse than an unbeliever" (1 Tim. 5:8). This is also presupposed when God tells Abraham that he will "command his children and his household after him, that they may keep the way of the Lord" (Gen. 18:19).

(3.) However, neither what we learn for ourselves nor what others teach us can do us any good if wickedness and malice have taken deep root. If neither divine nor human teaching could stop the shedding of blood when there was only one family in the world, how could there not be envy, strife, discord, and violence when families multiplied and increased on the earth? Has not nature given man intelligence and courage which, like armor, he can choose to use just as much for extreme evil as for good? Indeed did not the rest of the world use it to evil, while only Seth, Enoch, and their few descendants did otherwise? We all complain about the evils of our times, and not without reason, since the days are evil. But compare them with the times in which there were no political societies or any established public order, and in which only eight righteous people lived on the face of the earth, and we have very good reason to remember that God has greatly blessed us and made us live to see happy days indeed.

(4.) The only way for men to prevent quarrels, injuries, and wrongs was to come to a general agreement, creating some sort of government and subjecting themselves to it. Those to whom they granted authority to rule and govern were to procure the peace, tranquility, and happiness of the rest. Men always knew that they could defend themselves if someone attacked them. They also knew that men must not be allowed to pursue their own gain at the expense of others, and that such exploitation must instead be resisted by any reasonable means. Finally, they knew that no one should be the judge and defender of his own rights, since everyone is partial to himself and his closest friends, and therefore that conflict would never end unless all agreed by common consent to appoint one man as their judge. Without such consent, no one can justly become the lord or judge of another. Even though some very great and astute thinkers have said that noble, wise, and virtuous men have a natural right to govern those of more servile disposition, nonetheless the assent of those who are to be

LAWS BY WHICH POLITICAL SOCIETIES ARE GOVERNED

governed is necessary so that this right might be publicly acknowledged and so that both those who govern and the governed may be more at peace with one another.[1]

Nature gives supreme power to fathers within their families, which is why throughout all history we see that men have always been acknowledged as lords and lawful kings within their households. However, in a whole multitude, which is not dependent in the same way upon a single person and consists of many families, it is impossible for anyone to have complete lawful power without the consent of men or the appointment of God. After all, since men do not have a natural superiority over one another, as fathers have over children, such power would be usurped and unlawful unless it be granted to them by those over whom they exercise their authority, or unless this power be given to them by God, to whom the whole world is subject. Aristotle was probably correct when he said that the greatest in a household is always like a king, so when households joined together as a political society, kings were the first governors among them.[2] This is also, it seems to me, the reason why they often continued to be called fathers, since they were chosen from among fathers. This might also explain why the oldest kings were priests, like Melchizedek, a function which also belonged originally to fathers.

Nonetheless, this is not the only kind of government that has been received in the world, and in fact the inconveniences of monarchy have caused all the other kinds of

---

[1] Aristotle makes this distinction between the servile and dominating in *Politics* 1 and 4 [1255a and 1295b].

[2] Aristotle, *Politics* 1.2 [1252a].

DIVINE LAW AND HUMAN NATURE

government to be devised. In short, all public order has obviously come from careful advice, discussion, and agreement among men considering what is convenient and proper. It is possible that men before the Fall might have lived without any political organization, but given that our nature has been corrupted, we dare not deny that the law of nature now requires some form of government and that if we were to try to return to how things were at the beginning and to take away all public government, it would be the undoing of the world.

(5.) Things being as they are, the law of nature demands some kind of government, but there are many different kinds, and nature does not obligate us to any particular form, but leaves it up to human decision. When some sort of government was first agreed to, it may be that all was left to the wisdom and discretion of the rulers, with few limits on how they were to govern. However, by experience they found such a government to be very troublesome, such that the cure was worse than the disease.[3] They saw that to live by one man's will became the cause of all men's misery. This made them write laws in which men might know what their duties were beforehand, as well as the penalties for failing to fulfill them. In the case of things either obviously good or evil, about which everyone agrees, there is no need for new laws. Therefore, the first sort of law concerns things that are naturally good or evil, but are not readily discerned by every man's judgment without deeper consideration. Since it is possible to make a mistake in such considerations, many men would remain ignorant of their duties, or else pretend ignorance, which

---

[3] See Cicero, *De Officiis* 2.12.

LAWS BY WHICH POLITICAL SOCIETIES ARE GOVERNED

they cannot do once their duties have been defined by law.

(6.) Furthermore, most men prefer their own interests before everything else, and prefer sensible goods to spiritual ones. The difficulties that come with doing good, and the pleasure that comes from doing the opposite, make men slower to good and quicker to evil, even when their duties are laid down by law. Therefore, men have always found it necessary to augment laws with rewards, which attract men to the good more than any difficulty deters them, and punishments, which deter men from the evil more than any pleasure attracts them. While it is true that virtue deserves reward and vice deserves punishment, the particular way virtue is rewarded or vice punished must be decided by the lawmakers. For instance, theft by nature warrants some punishment, but the exact punishment is a matter of positive law, and should be determined as lawmakers think best.

(7.) Natural laws are obligatory to all; positive laws are not. Setting aside those positive laws which men impose upon themselves, such as vows to God, contracts with other men, and so forth, let us consider what is involved in making positive laws for governing a society. Laws not only teach what is good, but also demand it, and as such they carry coercive force. Since to constrain men to anything detrimental is unreasonable, it is essential that only wise men should devise laws which men are going to be forced to obey. Laws are matters of great importance, and men of ordinary abilities are not able to know—indeed how could they?—what things are most appropriate for each kind of government. We must recognize how much our obedience to our laws depends on this. If you correct anyone who is behaving in a disorderly fashion, observe how they take it. Who would not rage and storm at such correction and despise anyone that tries to reform them? However, the very people who cannot stand hearing of their duties from another man, will not hesitate to agree when they hear them proclaimed by law. Why do they do this? They know that laws are indifferent and impartial; they respect such laws as oracles of wisdom and understanding.

(8.) However, laws do not derive their coercive force from the wisdom of those that devise them, but from that power that gives them the strength of laws. What we said earlier about the power of government must also be applied here to the power of making laws. God has a power over all things, and by his natural law He has given to political societies the power of making laws to govern themselves. Indeed, if any prince or ruler of any kind tries to exercise this power without either an expressly received command from God, or without authority derived from the consent of the people he governs, he is nothing more than a tyrant.

Where there is no public consent, there is no law. However, this public consent happens not merely when an individual declares his assent by voice, sign, or act, but when another, rightfully designated to act on his behalf, does so in his stead. Even though we are not ourselves present in parliaments, councils, and similar assemblies, nonetheless we assent through agents acting there in our place, and what we do by others binds us no less than if we had been there for ourselves and done it in person. We often give our assent to many things without knowing, since the manner of our assenting is not obvious. For example, when an absolute monarch commands his subjects to do what seems good to him, is not his edict a law, whether they approve of it or not? Or consider those things that have been received by long custom, which we now obey as inviolable laws, even though our consent was never asked for.

We must repeat here our earlier point that, since men do not by nature have the power to command multitudes of men, we cannot be subject to any man's commands without at least some kind of consent. And we do consent to be commanded whenever the society we belong to has previously consented and has not revoked this consent by some universal agreement. Just as any man's past deed belongs to him as long as he lives, so also the act of a public society of men done five hundred years ago continues to belong to it, since societies are immortal. We lived in those who went before us, and they continue to live in those who follow them. Therefore, human laws, whatever kind they may be, have their force by consent.

(9.) If we ask here how, since all these things are common to all laws, we still witness such variety even in good laws, we must remember that we are dealing with many different purposes applied to many different circumstances, which require different sorts of laws. It is said there was a Greek law made by Pittacus which said that if anyone overcome with drink were to strike someone, he should be punished twice as much as if he had been sober.[4] This could hardly be deemed reasonable if we considered only the severity of the deed itself, since it is clearly worse to inflict harm intentionally than thoughtlessly. But in that society men,

---

[4] Aristotle, *Politics* 2.12 [1274b].

knowing that they could more easily get away with it, tended to brawl more often when they were drunk; therefore they clearly needed a positive law of this sort to remedy the situation. It is a law for law-makers that not all laws are right for every different society, and law-makers must be mindful of the place they live and the people they govern. For instance, wherever the multitude rules, minor government offices should be chosen by lot to avoid strife and division. After all, since such jobs require no great expertise, many will clamor for them and begrudge others the honor of receiving them, but selection by lot removes any cause of offense. High offices, which few are capable of, should be filled by popular election, since the masses can hardly envy those whom they themselves have appointed, and since those who win high office will spare no effort in exercising virtue to win the respect of their people. On the other hand, if the government is in the hands of the wealthiest, then the laws should make sharp penalties against them insulting and abusing the common people, lest the poor, who care little about holding high office but much about their basic human dignity, come to hate the rich for contemptuously treading upon them. Similarly, other types of government demand still other sorts of positive laws, which by their very nature cannot be the same everywhere.

(10.) As those who know the laws of our land point out, our statutes sometimes merely affirm or ratify what was previously prescribed by common law.[5] We must remember that all human laws written to order public societies

---

[5] Staunford, preface to *The Pleas of the Crown* [London: Richard Tottell, 1557]. There is a reprint from Professional Books, published in 1971.

must either establish some duty which all men had to obey before, or some duty which did not exist before. For distinction's sake, we may call the first sort *partly human* and the second sort *purely human*. It may sometimes be necessary to ratify by law that which plain and necessary reason already demands. For example, if a corrupt custom, such as incest or polygamy, has so far prevailed in a society that right reason has been wholly obscured, there is no way left to rectify such foul disorder except by law. Perhaps they no longer discern the clear dictates of reason; perhaps, like those the Apostle Jude laments, "whatever they know naturally, like brute beasts, in these things they corrupt themselves" (Jude 10); or perhaps merely, under the sway of their sensual desires, they are only likely to shun sin if painful punishments follow it; whatever the case, in such societies it will be necessary for the law to enforce what reason already teaches. We call these sorts of laws *partly human laws*, because they bind to the same matter as the law of reason, only in a different manner. Before the law was made, men were still constrained by conscience to obey the judgment of reason, but now they are constrained by law and, if they violate it, they may be punished. *Purely human* laws concern matters which seem prudent and beneficial according to probable reasoning. For example, in some places lands are inherited and divided between many children after the owner dies, whereas in other places only the eldest son inherits. If the law of reason necessarily required one of these two practices, then woe to those who do the opposite; reason would declare such a decree to be wicked, unjust, and unreasonable. However, neither of these things violates the law of reason, since it is likely that either of these options might be expedient, and only probable arguments can be found to support either.

(11.) Laws, whether partly or purely human, are made by political societies: some only as they are civilly united, some as they are spiritually joined and make up a body which we call the church. We will discuss laws governing the church in Book Three. Suffice it to say, Almighty God has graciously made us able to learn the laws which all men are always obligated to obey, and also those which are most beneficial for those who lead their lives under any ordered government.

(12.) Besides the laws which have to do with men as individuals and as members of some sort of political society, there is a third sort of law having to do with all political societies that have diplomatic relations with one another. This third sort is the Law of Nations. Men and beasts cannot have fellowship with one another because for men such fellowship necessarily includes sharing the fruits of our highest human faculties, and the primary way men have fellowship with others is through speech, since that is how we use our common reason to exchange thoughts.[6] Since beasts cannot do this and thus we cannot truly talk with them, they do not rise to the level of being man's associates, even though they are above things that do not have sense perception. This is why it says that "for man there was not found a help meet for him" (Gen. 2:20). Thus civil society is more proper for the nature of man than a hermit's life, so great is this good of mutual participation. Even then this is usually not enough, and we wish to have fellowship with all mankind; this is what Socrates

---

[6] See Aristotle, *Politics* 1.2 [1253a].

was talking about when he called himself a citizen, not of any particular commonwealth, but of the world.[7] A clear proof of this desire for universal fellowship appears in the fact that men so much enjoy visiting foreign countries or learning about nations previously unheard of. We all wish to know the affairs and dealings of other peoples and to be in a league of friendship with them, not only for the sake of trade or to build strength through alliances, but also for the very reason that the Queen of Sheba visited Solomon; we cannot help but think that the great variety of men in the world are, as it were, to us so many gods, to be honored and sought out accordingly.

(13) Concerning laws which are to serve man for mutual commerce between societies, here too we find that, as with the law of reason governing men as individuals and governing particular nations, what would have served man well enough before the Fall, is hardly sufficient for a corrupt and fallen race so prone to violence. This is the root of the distinction between *primary* and *secondary* laws, the former dealing with our original nature, and the latter with our depraved nature. *Primary laws* of nations concern embassies, hospitality towards foreigners and strangers, good trade, and so on. *Secondary laws* are those this troubled world knows only too well, especially laws of arms, which are better known than kept. However, I will not discuss here in any detail what the law of nations contains.

This unwritten law of nations cannot be overturned by any particular nation's laws and ordinances, any more than an

---

[7] Quoted in Plutarch's *Of Banishment*. See Plutarch, *Plutarch's Moralia VII*, trans. Phillip H. De Lacy and Benedict Einarson, Loeb Classical Library 405 (Cambridge, MA: Harvard University Press, 1959), 601.

individual can overturn the laws of his native commonwealth and government. Since civil law is an act performed by the whole body politic and overrules all individuals within it, in the same way no particular commonwealth has the right to unilaterally reject what the whole world has implicitly agreed upon. This is why, for instance, Josephus and Theodoret rightly fault the Spartans for denying all access to their shores, an affront to the hospitality which all nations should practice for the sake their common humanity.[8]

(14). Now, just as we need laws to maintain fellowship among the nations, so also among Christian nations something similar is needed for the sake of our communion in the faith. Among such nations, general councils have authority. Just as in the essentials of the faith, there is one divine law that serves as a rule to all Christian churches, making us in this respect a single church with "one Lord, one faith, one baptism" (Eph. 4:5), so likewise, the Church of God on earth needs some laws to maintain outward unity between Christian nations, both in these essentials and also in secondary matters where uniformity would be helpful. These laws enable churches to make use of those reverend, religious, and sacred assemblies, which we call general councils. Assemblies of this sort were inspired by the Holy Spirit Himself (Acts 15:28), and practiced by the holy Apostles; indeed, the general council was highly esteemed by all until pride, ambition, and tyranny began to use God's gift to advance wicked schemes. However, just as the authority of courts and parliaments is not abolished,

---

[8] Josephus, *Against Apion* 2.36; and Theodoret, *Cure of the Affections of the Greeks* 9.

LAWS BY WHICH POLITICAL SOCIETIES ARE GOVERNED

even though men in power twist them to selfish ends, so the abuse of councils should not make us discard them, but rather push us to carefully consider how so beneficial a thing can be restored to its original perfection.

Space will not permit me to do full justice to this important matter. For now, this is all I have to say: whether we are seeking the truth about some essential of the faith where men are not yet fully agreed, or establishing uniform practice in a secondary matter where open discord causes offense and scandal; whether we are seeking to resolve disputes about Christian belief in which each side has good arguments, or we are talking about matters of church government and order—in any case, I have no doubt that all Christians would better obey our Lord and Savior's commands to peace and unity if we were committed to restoring the ancient practice of church councils, rather than continuing in endless debates or ending them in the worst possible way: by the sword.

(15.) Now that this foundation has been laid, let us go on to discuss why God has made known in Scripture laws for the direction of men.

11
WHY GOD HAS MADE KNOWN IN SCRIPTURE SUPERNATURAL LAWS TO DIRECT MEN'S STEPS

(1.) EVERYTHING, except for God, is not so perfect within itself that it cannot be improved by something outside itself, as we have already shown. After all, there is nothing in the world, whether great or small, for which our knowing it or using it might not add a little to our perfection. Whatever can make our nature more perfect, we call our *good*. Our greatest good or beatitude is when we reach such a degree of perfection that there is nothing left to wish for; we are so content and satisfied with it that we rejoice in what we have and thirst for nothing more. Other kinds of good things are not desired for their own sake, but only because they are means to something else, such as money. Finally, other kinds of good such as health, virtue, and knowledge are genuinely desired for their own sake, yet they are not the final goal of all our endeavors, but still point beyond themselves; we may enjoy such goods and yet continue to desire something more. All these different kinds of good are connected and intertwined with one another: we work to eat and we eat to live and we live to do good and we do good for the sake of a future harvest (cf. Gal. 6:8). At some point, however, we must stop. After all, if everything were desired for something else *ad infinitum*, our actions would be without purpose and we would not know where we were going; all would be in vain. Just as to take away our first cause would take away our existence, so also to take away the final goal of all our labor would cause all work to cease. Therefore, something must be desired for its own sake alone. Indeed, for such a thing, it would be perverse to desire it for the sake of anything beyond itself. To be sure, oxen desire their food and have no deeper motive, so that for them food is desired for its own sake. But this is because their imperfection prevents them from desiring anything further. Contrast this with that which has so excellent a nature that it *cannot* be desired for some further end.

(2.) Now whatever a man desires for the sake of something else, he will desire only as much as he needs for the sake of that end. However, what he desires as good in and of itself, towards that his desire is infinite. So unless the good we desire for its own sake is also infinite, we do evil when we make it our final good. This is what happens when we place our hopes in wealth or honor or pleasure or anything we can achieve in this life, since it is a grievous error to desire anything as our final perfection which is not. No good should be infinitely desired, except for one that is infinite itself. The better the good is, the more we should desire it, and that which is infinitely good we should desire most of all. If anything we desire is infinite, it must be the best of all things to be desired. No good is infinite except

God, and therefore He alone is our happiness and bliss. Furthermore, desire is always drawn to union with what it desires. If then we are blessed in Him, it is by partaking of Him and being joined to Him. Again, it is not the mere possession of some good that makes anyone happy, but actively enjoying it. Then we are happy when we fully enjoy God as an object which satisfies our souls with everlasting delight so that although we are men, yet in a manner of speaking, by union with God we live the life of God.

(3.) Happiness is therefore that condition in which we come to possess as much as possible that which is desired for its own sake and fully contains within itself the fulfillment of our desires, which is our highest possible perfection. We are not able to reach such perfection in this life, since while we are in the world we are subject to countless imperfections, bodily pains, and defects of mind. Indeed, even the best things we can do are painful and it is laborious to continue in them, so that we cannot complete those actions in which we find the highest fulfillment of our nature, but are often forced by weariness to come to a halt. But when our union with God is complete, and we are in the state of bliss, we will no longer experience such tedious striving. Complete union with Him must involve every faculty of our mind that is suitable for receiving so glorious an object. We are capable of enjoying God both through our understanding and through our will: through our understanding inasmuch as He is the sovereign Truth who contains in Himself all treasures of wisdom, and through our will inasmuch as He is that sea of Goodness, that whoever drinks of it will thirst no more. Whatever the will does not now possess, it pursues by a desire or sense of

WHY GOD HAS MADE KNOWN SUPERNATURAL LAWS

lack, but once it does possess it, it clings to it by love. St. Augustine says that the desire of those who thirsted is changed into the sweet enjoyment of those who have tasted and are satisfied.[1] Whereas we now love what is good especially because it benefits us, we shall then love it solely (or primarily) for the sake of its own goodness and beauty. Our souls will then be perfected not only with love of that infinite good, but also with the supernatural passions of joy, peace, and delight. All this is endless and everlasting: our blessedness is called "the crown of glory that fadeth not away" (1 Pet. 5:4). This perpetuity comes not from the crown itself or from the nature of our souls; it rests alone in the will of God, which perfects our nature to this high degree and continues it in such perfection.

Creatures lower than man are not capable of joy and bliss. There are two reasons for this: first, their perfection is limited to what is best for them, and does not extend to what is best in itself, as it does for us; and second, whatever perfection they may achieve does not transcend their nature, as ours does. In light of this, how fitting are the words of the Prophet in his admiration of the goodness of God, "What is man, that Thou makest him to have dominion over the works of thy hands" (Ps. 8:4, 6) so that you are the end of all his strivings and the sum of his delight.

(4.) Now, if this desire to be happy were not natural, then why do all men have this desire? Since all men do have it, this desire must be natural; we cannot help it. And how

---

[1] Hill renders it "the same love with which one longs open-mouthed to know a thing becomes love of the thing known when it holds and embraces the acceptable offspring." Augustine, *On the Trinity*, trans. Edmund Hill (New York: New City Press, 1991), 285 [9.3].

could we be apathetic about it? Is not this natural desire greater than anything else man feels? And is it likely that God would make the hearts of men so yearn for something which they could never have? It is an axiom of nature that no natural desire is utterly incapable of fulfillment.[2] This desire would be completely pointless if it could never be satisfied.

Man seeks a threefold perfection: first, he seeks a physical satisfaction, pursuing things which are necessary for life itself, and such things which merely adorn or enhance it; second, an intellectual satisfaction, pursuing things that creatures lower than him cannot understand or experience at all; and third, a spiritual and divine satisfaction, consisting of the things which we seek by supernatural grace, but cannot fully attain in this life. Those who are only interested in the first, the Apostle says, are those whose god is their belly, and who are earthly-minded men (Phil. 3:19). Those who seek intellectual fulfillment pursue the sort of knowledge and virtue that brings honor to man. This type of happiness includes the attainment of moral and civil virtues. To show that there must be something beyond this, we only need to remember that man's desire would languish unfulfilled if it stopped here, desiring as it does an infinite happiness which no finite thing can offer. For man is not content either with mere physical continuance, or with such things as win the praise of men. He longs, even hungers and thirsts for a food which cannot sustain the body or satisfy the senses, something even beyond the capacity of his reason. He seeks something divine and

---

[2] Aquinas, *Commentary on Aristotle's Metaphysics*, trans. John P. Rowan (Chicago: Regnery, 1961), 1:8 [Prologue 2].

WHY GOD HAS MADE KNOWN SUPERNATURAL LAWS

heavenly, which he can more guess at than conceive. He seeks for it, and although he does not know exactly what it is, yet his desire is so great that he sets aside all other delights and pleasures to find what he merely dreams of. If man's soul only served to give him physical life, then he would be satisfied with those things that sustain his life, as are other creatures who seek nothing further and have no greater purpose. But it is not so with us. Even if a single man had all the beauty, riches, honors, knowledge, virtues, and perfections possessed by all men, he would still seek and thirst for something more. Even in this life, then, our nature demands a more divine perfection.

(5.) This last and highest condition of perfection which we are discussing is received by men as a *reward*. Rewards always presuppose the doing of duties which are rewardable. The natural means to achieve this blessedness then would be through our works, and indeed the natural mind could never discover any other means of salvation. However, if we consider the works that we do, what man has ever been born who can say, "My ways are pure?" Since all flesh is guilty of doing things that God has promised to eternally punish, what hope is there for us to be saved this way? Therefore if there is any way to achieve salvation it must be supernatural. The heart of man could never conceive or imagine such a thing unless God Himself revealed it to us supernaturally. This is why we call it the mystery of salvation.

St. Ambrose rightly looks to God and not to man: "Let God Himself, Who made me, teach me the mystery of heaven, not man, who knew not himself."³ Lactantius says,

> Whenever men of great and excellent character gave themselves completely to a doctrine, they bore whatever labor could be expended in despising all things, even private and public concerns, for the pursuit of searching after the truth. It was their full belief that to reason of things human and divine was much more splendid than to cling to the amassing of wealth and accumulation of honors.... But they never arrived at that at which they wished ... because truth, that is, the secret of the supreme God who made all things, is not able to be comprehended by [human] ability and its proper senses. Otherwise there would be no distance between God and man if human thought could attain to the counsels and dispositions of that eternal majesty. But, since it could not be that the divine plan should become known to man of himself, God did not allow man seeking the light of wisdom to be in error any longer and to wander without any effect of his labor through inextricable darkness. He opened his eyes then and made the knowledge of the truth His gift, so that He might show that even human wisdom was nothing, and He pointed out the way of gaining immortality to the erring and wandering one.⁴

Lactantius Firmianus here shows that God Himself is the

---

³ Ambrose, *Epistle 18.7*, in *Nicene and Post-Nicene Fathers*, vol. 10, *Ambrose: Select Works and Letters*, ed. Philip Schaff and Henry Wace (1896; Peabody, MA: Hendrickson Publishers, 1995), 418.

⁴ Lactantius, *The Divine Institutes: Books I-VII* (Washington, DC: Catholic University of America Press, 1964), 15-16 [1.1].

WHY GOD HAS MADE KNOWN SUPERNATURAL LAWS

teacher of the truth by which we know the supernatural way of salvation and the law in which those who will be saved must live. The natural way to everlasting life begins with the ability to do good, as man could do when God created him, such that man was to obey His creator with complete righteousness and sincerity in all his actions, and then at the end, God in his justice would reward the worthiness of his deeds with a crown of eternal glory. If Adam had continued in this original condition, this would have been the way of life for him and all his descendants. Nonetheless, I agree with Duns Scotus that "if we speak of strict justice, God could not have been bound in any way to reward man's labors in so full a way as human happiness would wish for, inasmuch as such supreme happiness so far exceeds the value of any human labor. But we can say that God out of his great liberality had determined on account of man's endeavors to bestow such happiness by the rule of that justice that most suited him—the justice of one who rewards nothing stingily, but in rich and overflowing measure. Still, even from this it could never be concluded that God would make that reward an everlasting one, since even a momentary possession of bliss would be for us greater reward than our labors could ever deserve."[5] However, we are not going to ask further how gracious and bountiful our God would be in rewarding the sons of men, had they perfectly obeyed whatever they were obligated to do. Regardless of how we understand this reward, we needed to obey to be rewarded, and having

---

[5] *Questions on the Four Books of Sentences of Peter Lombard*, Bk. 4, dist. 49, q. 6 in *Opera Ioannis Duns Scoti* (Civitas Vaticana: Typis Polyglottis Vaticanis, 1950), 1:59-87. (Here, we have used Hooker's own translation, modernized appropriately.)

failed to obey, we forfeited the reward. The light of nature cannot show us any way to receive the reward of bliss except by perfectly carrying out the duties and works of righteousness.

(6.) Since all flesh therefore cannot attain by natural means to salvation and life, behold how the wisdom of God has revealed a hidden and supernatural way that directs us to this same life. This way presupposes the guiltiness of sin and our just reward of condemnation and death. This way begins with the compassion of God towards those of us who are drowned and swallowed up in misery, according to which He redeems us from this misery through the precious death and merit of our mighty Savior, who has said that He is the way that leads us out of bondage into bliss. This supernatural way God Himself prepared before all worlds and commanded by our Savior in the Gospel of John: "This is the work of God, that ye believe on Him whom He hath sent" (Jn. 6:29). This is not because God requires nothing from man but mere naked belief, for we must not exclude hope and love, but because without faith all other things are as nothing, and faith is the foundation of all other virtues. The highest object of faith is the eternal truth which has discovered the treasures of hidden wisdom in Christ; the highest object of hope is the everlasting goodness which in Christ quickens the dead; the highest object of love is the incomprehensible beauty which shines in the countenance of Christ, the Son of the living God. Faith begins in this life with a frail apprehension of things not seen, and ends with the immediate vision of God in the world to come; hope begins with a trembling expectation of things far removed and only known by report, and ends with the attainment of such

WHY GOD HAS MADE KNOWN SUPERNATURAL LAWS

things as no tongue can express; love begins here with a weak inclination of the heart towards Him whom we cannot approach, and ends with endless union, a mystery which is higher than the reach of the minds of men. Of these three—without which there can be no salvation—where besides Scripture would we have ever learned of them? Not a true syllable has ever been uttered about any of these three that has not been supernaturally revealed from the mouth of the eternal God!

Therefore laws concerning these things are supernatural, both in how they are delivered, which is divine, and in what they deliver, which could never have originated from nature alone. For God, acting outside the course of nature, freely ordained these laws to bring nature back to her proper course.

12
WHY SO MANY NATURAL LAWS AND LAWS OF REASON ARE FOUND IN SCRIPTURE

(1.) WHEN supernatural duties are required, natural duties are not rejected as needless. Even though the Law of God is principally delivered to teach us the former, yet it is suffused with the latter as well. Scripture is shot through with the laws of Nature, so much so that Gratian describes Natural Right (the right which naturally obligates men as they are men) as that which is contained in the Books of the Law and the Gospel.[1] Nor is it in vain that the Scripture abounds with so many laws of this kind. Scripture does this because they are either such as we could not easily have found out on our own, or because, in cases when they are obvious, the Spirit may set them down in Scripture in order to prove things more obscure, and this application of the laws of nature to difficult particular cases is of great value for our instruction. Besides, whether or not they are plain in themselves or difficult, God's own

---

[1] Gratian, *Decretum*, in *Corpus juris canonici*, 1:1 [preface].

WHY MANY NATURAL LAWS ARE FOUND IN SCRIPTURE

testimony added to our reason strengthens our confidence and confirms our conclusions.

(2.) Therefore, since in this life we face many different circumstances and thus come to many different conclusions about what we should do, it is necessary that divine law should condescend to our weakness so that we might better understand what is good and what is evil. The first principles of the Law of Nature are easy; indeed, it would be difficult to find men ignorant of them. However, when it comes to particular applications of this law, so far has our natural understanding been darkened that at times whole nations have been unable to recognize even gross iniquity as sin. Again, we are inclined to flatter ourselves and to learn as little about our defects as possible, and the less we know about them the less we desire to get rid of them. How shall these festering sores be cured if God did not deliver a law as sharp as a two-edged sword, piercing the deepest and most unsearchable corners of the heart, which the Law of Nature can scarcely reach, and human laws not at all? By this law, we know even secret lusts to be sinful and we fear to sin, even in a wandering thought. Finally, there are many laws necessary to direct our lives which, although they could in principle be discovered, few men with natural capacity have ever found them out—indeed, some have never been discovered. St. Augustine notes that few are wise and clever enough, few free enough from all distractions, few sufficiently instructed in the higher points of learning, to have discovered even the immortality of the soul. And did any man ever guess the resurrection of the flesh from the school of Nature alone?[2]

---

[2] This claim—that the resurrection of the body could even *in principle* be

Therefore we should yield eternal thanks to our Creator, the Father of all mercy, for delivering His law to the world, a law in which so many things are made plain, clear, and obvious, which otherwise would have lain hidden, to the ruin of many thousands of souls that now by God's grace are saved.

(3.) We see then that our greatest good is naturally desired, and that God the author of that natural desire appointed a natural means to fulfill it, but that man by sin has rendered his nature unable to follow this path, so God has revealed to him a law whereby what he desires naturally must now be achieved supernaturally. Finally, we see that since supernatural duties do not exclude natural ones as unnecessary, therefore the same law teaches, along with the supernatural duties that could not otherwise be known, natural duties which are difficult to discover through nature alone.

---

knowable by mere natural reason—seems at first bewildering, given what a distinctively Christian doctrine this seems to be. However, Hooker here seems to be following the reasoning of Thomas Aquinas, who argues as follows in his *Summa Contra Gentiles* Bk. IV, Q. 79, sect. 10: "For we showed in Book II that the souls of men are immortal. They persist, then, after their bodies, released from their bodies. It is also clear from what was said in Book II that the soul is naturally united to the body, for in its essence it is the form of the body. It, then, contrary to the nature of the soul to be without the body. But nothing which is contrary to nature can be perpetual. Perpetually, then, the soul will not be without the body. Since, then, it persists perpetually, it must once again be united to the body; and this is to rise again. Therefore, the immortality of souls seems to demand a future resurrection of bodies" (translated by Charles O'Neil, edited by Joseph Kenny, O.P. [New York: Hanover House, 1955-57]; available at http://dhspriory.org/thomas/ContraGentiles4.htm).

13
THE ADVANTAGE OF HAVING SUCH DIVINE LAWS WRITTEN

(1.) IN THE first age of the world, God gave laws to our fathers, and because they lived so long their memories served instead of books, but since God knew their shortcomings, He mercifully reminded them of what they most needed to remember. Thus we find God sometimes repeating similar teachings over and over again even to the wisest amongst them. After men's lives were shortened, God gave men a more reliable means of preserving His laws. It is said therefore of Moses that he "wrote all the words of the Lord" (Ex. 24:4), not of his own devising, since God attributes this writing to Himself: "I have written" (Ex. 24:12). Were not the Prophets who came afterwards commanded to do the same? So also St. John is expressly charged, "Write these things" (e.g., Rev. 1:11; 14:13). St. Augustine says of the rest of our Lord's disciples, "For all that he was minded to give for our perusal on the subject of His own doings and sayings, He commanded to be committed by His disciples, whom He thus used as if they were His own hands."[1]

(2.) Of course, it is not essential that the law of God be written; writing these laws down does not add authority and strength to them, and His laws demand the same obedience regardless of how they are delivered. Nonetheless, who can help admiring and praising His providence in delivering them to us in this way? The setting down of God's Word in writing has been of inestimable value to the world. If we are asked whether we should seek for God's laws somewhere other than in sacred Scripture, and offer the same obedience and reverence to the traditions thrust upon us by the Church of Rome, honoring them as divine, then the answer is No! As for those who so zealously argue for the authority of tradition, as if oral report was the most reliable means of transmitting truths from generation to generation, it seems miraculous that they could be so deceived. If they are so simple-minded, perhaps we should leave them to the enjoyment of their "truths." But they cannot possibly be ignorant what danger the truth is in, how maimed and deformed it becomes, when it is conveyed by oral report. Let those who think this merely consider the fate of those few divine truths which the pagans received in this way.[2] How miserable would the Church of God be by now if, lacking Scripture, we had no record of His laws beyond what the memory of

---

[1] Augustine, *On the Harmony of the Gospels*, trans. S.D.F. Salmond ([San Bernardino, CA]: Aeterna Press, 2013), 46 [1.54].

[2] Hooker's footnote: "I refer to those historical matters concerning the condition of the antediluvian world, the flood, the sons of Noah, the Exodus, the life and deeds of Moses, and so forth; the certain truth, delivered in holy scripture, appears in pagan legends only by oral report, and it is so mixed with fantastical myths that all that remains are the barely visible tracks of the truth."

THE ADVANTAGE OF HAVING DIVINE LAWS WRITTEN

man received by report from his predecessors!

(3.) God in His wisdom has seen fit to deliver to the world by Scripture many things that concern particular duties of particular men; many deep and profound points of doctrine upon which these duties depend; many prophecies which when fulfilled might confirm men in things unseen; many stories that are mirrors in which we see the faithfulness of God to all those who devoutly serve, obey, and honor Him; many examples of piety as patterns and models for those in similar circumstances; many things by way of explication; and many things by way of application to particular occasions—all of these God has provided in the books of Scripture. Along with all the most necessary laws of God, Scripture includes many other diverse things, which we could be ignorant of and yet be saved. But shall we then think them superfluous? Shall we consider them as wayward shoots obscuring more pleasant and fruitful vines? No more so than we would consider our hands and our eyes, without which we would still remain completely human. Just as a complete man does not lack anything necessary, but also has many parts not strictly necessary which nonetheless are of great use to him in their own way, in the same way all the writings which contain the Law of God, all those hallowed books of Scripture, all those sacred volumes of Holy Writ are composed with such absolute perfection that they neither lack anything that would deprive us of salvation, nor do they abound with anything that is superfluous, unfruitful, or altogether needless.

14
THE SUFFICIENCY OF SCRIPTURE UNTO THE END FOR WHICH IT WAS INSTITUTED

(1.) ALTHOUGH Scripture is a storehouse of infinite treasures, abounding with many sorts of laws, its principal intent is to reveal to us our supernatural duties. There have been many deep discussions about whether everything necessary for salvation is necessarily found in Scripture or not. If we define "necessary for salvation" as anything that makes the way to salvation more plain, apparent, and obvious, then we cannot exclude any philosophy, art, or science of note from the things Scripture must contain. But let us define things necessary for salvation as only those beliefs and actions without which God does not ordinarily grant salvation.

It may then be asked (and in fact it has been asked many times[1]) if the books of Holy Scripture contain everything

---

[1] *Questions on the Four Books of Sentences of Peter Lombard*, in *Ioannis Duns Scoti Opera Omnia* (Civitas Vaticana: Typis Polyglottis Vaticanis, 1950), prologue, part 2 [1:59-87].

THE SUFFICIENCY OF SCRIPTURE UNTO ITS END

necessary, then how do we know which books count as Scripture? That is something we cannot get from Scripture itself, after all! We may truly reply that every field of study requires the prior knowledge of some things that lie outside that field of study properly speaking. Each kind of knowledge only goes so far and takes for granted many things supplied by other fields. For instance, whoever wishes to teach the art of eloquence must explain the rules necessary to reach this end. But, since no one can speak eloquently unless he can first speak in proper sentences, it would seem such basic ability is a necessary part of the art of eloquence. However, it would clearly be ridiculous for someone teaching oratory to try to teach elementary grammar. While his profession involves teaching what is necessary for eloquent speech, those whom he teaches must first learn much about speaking beforehand.

It is the same with Scripture. Even though Scripture says that it contains all things necessary for salvation, "all things" cannot be construed to mean absolutely "all things," but all things of a certain kind, such as all things which we could not know by our natural reason. Scripture does indeed contain all these things. However, it also presupposes that we first know and are persuaded of certain rational first principles, and building on that, Scripture teaches us the rest. Among the things we must first believe is the sacred authority of Scripture itself. Since we are persuaded by other means that the Scriptures are indeed the oracles of God, they teach us everything else we must know and do for salvation.

(2.) Furthermore, there is a similar question about whether "contained in Scripture" means it is specifically mentioned or whether it simply means that we may clearly deduce from Scripture all things that are necessary. We have already given several reasons to reject the former construal. After all, such doctrines as the Trinity, the co-eternity of the Son with the Father, the proceeding of the Spirit from the Father and the Son, the duty of baptizing infants, and others that no one denies to be necessary, are not expressly mentioned in Scripture, but are only deduced from comparing different parts of Scripture. On the other hand, when we define "contained in Scripture" this way, still we must ask ourselves how far we can take this process of deduction before we leave the realm of "things necessary." For the mind of man will never finish sounding the depths of all that may be gleaned from Scripture as long as the world endures, especially if "deduced from Scripture" is broad enough to include probable conjectures. However, if we are talking about what can be *necessarily* deduced from Scripture, then I deny that any of your proposals for reforming church-government fall under this heading, at least from what you have yet argued in all your books; I challenge you to name a single example of something necessarily deduced from Scripture which is not accepted by both sides.

(3.) We have already shown how things necessary for salvation must be potentially knowable by all men, and that many of these things cannot be known by the light of nature. From this it follows either that all flesh is excluded from hope of salvation—which would be an impious thought—or else that God has supernaturally revealed enough for us to discover the way of life. For this reason, God has in many times and ways spoken to mankind, and has instructed and taught His church not only by speech,

THE SUFFICIENCY OF SCRIPTURE UNTO ITS END

but also and especially by writing. He teaches this way so that what He reveals might last longer and be more certain, since what is recorded is so much better than what passes from man to man and has no pens save tongues and no books save the ears of men. Since each of the books of Scripture was written for a different occasion and purpose, depending on the need, each book of Scripture includes whatever natural, historical, foreign, and supernatural truths are necessary for the matter at hand.

So we can safely conclude that all things necessary for salvation must be specially made known to us, and that God Himself has therefore revealed His will—since otherwise men could not have known what was necessary. Therefore, His ceasing to speak to the world since the proclamation and writing down of the Gospel of Jesus Christ is a sign that the way of salvation is sufficiently proclaimed and that <u>nothing else is needed for our full instruction than what God has already given us.</u>

(4.) The main point of the whole New Testament is what John describes as the purpose of his own account: "these are written, that ye may believe that Jesus is the Christ, the Son of God; and that believing ye may have life in his name" (Jn. 20:31). The same is true of the Old Testament, as the Apostle tells Timothy, they are "able to make thee wise unto salvation" (2 Tim. 3:15). The only difference between the two is that the Old Testament made wise unto salvation by teaching salvation through the Christ who would come, while the New Testament teaches that Christ the Savior has come, and that the very Jesus whom the Jews crucified and whom God raised from the dead is He. When the Apostle therefore tells Timothy that the Old was able to make him wise unto salvation, he was not saying that the Old Testament alone does this for those who live after the New has come. For there he presupposes that Timothy knows the doctrine of Christ and therefore he says, "But abide thou in the things which thou hast learned and hast been assured of, knowing of whom thou hast learned them" (2 Tim. 3:14). He does admit that those Scriptures were able to make him wise to salvation, but he adds "through faith which is in Christ Jesus" (2 Tim. 3:15). Therefore, even though the Old Testament foreshadowed how Christ would accomplish the redemption of the world, without the teaching of the New Testament, it cannot save us. The Apostle assumes the New when he praises the Old. In the same way as Paul's words about the Scriptures presuppose the Gospel of Christ, so also when we praise the complete sufficiency of Scripture, we must be careful not to exclude the benefit of the light of nature just because we insist on the necessity of a more divine light.

(5.) There is nothing that prevents Scripture from enlightening a man's natural understanding, no matter what place or calling he holds within the Church of God, such that grace perfecting nature, he will lack no instruction in any good work which God requires, whether natural or supernatural, or whether concerning men as individuals or as members of society. Thus, we say that Nature and Scripture do serve us in such a way that neither alone are sufficient, but that both working jointly are so complete that we need nothing further to find eternal joy. Therefore those who add traditions as necessary supernatural truths, do not have the truth at all, but are in error. For they merely argue that we should receive whatever God reveals, by writing or otherwise, as necessary to all Christian men to do or believe, a thing which no one denies. But they who argue for this higher view of tradition must prove that such traditions are indeed inspired and divine. For we do not reject traditions as divine just because they are not in Scripture, but because they are neither in Scripture nor can they be proved by any other sufficient reason to be of God. We do not deny that even unwritten traditions, if they could be proved to be from God, would have the same force and authority as the written laws of God. We acknowledge that the Apostles instituted and ordained certain rites and customs for the sake of orderliness in the church, which rites and customs were not committed to writing.[2] However, these Apostolic rites and customs are changeable. We grant them no less weight than any other such changeable rites in the church, even those that are set down in the writings of the Apostles. For although both are Apostolic, it is not the way they are delivered to the church, but God from whom they spring that gives them force and credibility.

---

[2] William Whitaker, *Disputatio De Sacra Scriptura Whitaker against Bellarmine, contra R. Bellarminum and T. Stapletonum* [Cambridge: Thomas Thomas, 1588], 384 [question 6, section 6].

15
POSITIVE LAWS IN SCRIPTURE, HOW SOME OF THEM ARE CHANGEABLE, AND THE GENERAL USE OF SCRIPTURE

(1.) LAWS CAN be imposed either by a man upon himself, or by a society upon its members, or by all nations upon particular societies, or by the Lord Himself upon any of these. Each of these laws includes both those which we call natural laws and those which we call positive laws. It is a grave error to imagine that only human laws are positive, or to think that all positive laws are changeable. Natural laws always bind; positive laws, only when they have been expressly and intentionally imposed. Positive laws can be found in each of the four categories just mentioned. First, positive laws imposed by a man on himself include promises to one's neighbor and vows to God; these are laws that we tie ourselves to and until we have so tied ourselves, we have no obligations here. Second, positive laws imposed by a society upon its members are the civil laws that are distinctive to each commonwealth. Third, positive laws imposed by the nations on individual commonwealths would include such things as laws between nations concerning conduct in war. Fourth, positive laws imposed by the Lord Himself would include the judicial laws of the Old Covenant. Although only positive laws are changeable, this does not mean that all positive laws are. Positive laws can be either permanent or changeable, depending on what sort of subject matter they concern. It has nothing to do with whether they are made by God or man; they may be capable of change, as the matter which they govern requires.

(2.) All laws concerning supernatural duties are, in fact, positive laws, and either have to do with individual men as far as their souls are concerned, or as members of a supernatural society, the church. When we speak of "men as far as their souls are concerned," what we mean is that all men, as individual spiritual beings, have those same spiritual obligations which we could never have known unless God Himself had revealed them to us. They cannot be deduced from the natural order, but have been appointed by God since we can no longer attain to salvation by natural means. When speak of the church as a "supernatural society," we note that while other societies concern men simply as men, the church, being a spiritual body, consists of men as joined to God, angels, and all the saints. Even though the Church, inasmuch as it is a temporal society, is formed by much the same means as other temporal societies (by a natural inclination to sociable life and consent to rules regarding their bond of union), the Church, inasmuch as it is a *supernatural* society, has one unique feature: part of their bond of union is a supernatural law, which God has revealed concerning the sort of worship that His people should offer to Him. Therefore, the elements of the worship of God, inasmuch as they go beyond what reason teaches, may not be invented by men, as it is with the pagans, but must be received from God Himself, as it always has been with the Church when she has not forgotten her duty.

(3.) Therefore, let us end with a general rule for all the laws which God has required of men: all divinely commanded laws, whether natural or supernatural, whether dealing with men as individuals or as members of temporal societies or as members of that temporal society which is the church, all these laws are eternally binding, provided that we exclude all the changeable and incidental particulars which are always present in men, societies, and the church. This is because, when we consider the general subject matter of the law, the overall purpose for which it was instituted, this cannot be changed without cause, and there can be no cause for change if this underlying subject matter does not change. On the other hand, laws made with respect to those aspects of men or societies or churches that *are* prone to change—and sometimes to change completely—may be modified as needed. No man of common sense will deny that the laws of God which are of this latter, changeable sort are different from the former, unchanging type, and this seems to be the very reason why St. John calls the teaching of the salvation by Jesus Christ an eternal Gospel (Rev. 14:6), since as long as the world continues, there is no reason for ceasing to teach it or to proclaim another instead. By contrast, all the laws of Old Covenant rites and ceremonies, though delivered with great solemnity, have been utterly abolished since God only had a temporary reason for ordaining them.

POSITIVE LAWS IN SCRIPTURE

(4.) However, let us conclude this introduction to the nature and origin of laws found in Scripture, whose author is God, whom even the infidels agree can neither mistake nor deceive.[1] Nonetheless, some things are so clear and obvious to all men by common sense that we do not even need to consult Scripture for them. For just as a man admired for wisdom would think it beneath him to be consulted about a trifle, so some things are so insignificant that it would be disrespectful to the dignity of Scripture to seek to prove them by Biblical prooftexts.

To be sure, it would be much better to be over-scrupulous in this way than to be profane, and make even the weightiest decisions in life with no reference to the Word of God. Concerning the custom of the pagans themselves, Strabo testifies that men

> exist in a political community and live under common decrees, for otherwise it would not be possible for the masses to do any single thing joined together with each other—which is what it is to be a citizen—or to live a common life in any other way. The decrees are double, from God and from mankind. Those in antiquity worshipped and honored the gods more, and because of this, those who consulted oracles at that time were numerous.[2]

If they paid so much attention to the voices of their gods, who in truth were no gods at all, how much more should we consult with the oracles of the true and living God, a

---

[1] Plato, *Republic* 2 [382E].

[2] *The Geography of Strabo: An Introduction, with Introduction and Notes*, trans. Duane W. Roller (Cambridge: CUP, 2014) [16.38].

rich store to which He has given us free and easy access! As David confesses to God, "Thy commandments make me wiser than mine enemies; for they are ever with me. I have more understanding than all my teachers; for thy testimonies are my meditation" (Ps. 119:98-99). Imagine how eagerly those who traveled sea and land to glean wisdom from renowned sages would have devoted themselves to the study of these books. The pagans were astounded by what little they happened to hear about the wisdom contained in Scripture.[3] Whenever they talk of such divine truths, they speak strangely and not as they do elsewhere, but they themselves admit that their great wits were conquered by the profundity of these truths. God has given us our senses so that we might perceive those things on which our physical life depends; He has given us reason so that we might know what is necessary for both our present and future state; and He has opened to us with prophetic revelation the hidden mysteries that reason could never have unlocked or shown to be so necessary for our everlasting good. Therefore let us use the precious gifts that God has given us, for His glory and honor, seeking to know by every means possible what His will is, what is righteous before Him, and what is holy, perfect, and good in His sight so that we may truly and faithfully do it.

---

[3] Hooker is referring to the *Songs of Orpheus*, in the same fashion as Justin Martyr, *Exhortation to the Greeks* 15 and Eusebius, *Evangelical Preparation* 9.27 and 13.12.

16
CONCLUSION:
HOW ALL OF THIS PERTAINS TO THE PRESENT CONTROVERSY

(1.) SO FAR we have tried to show what the nature and force of laws are, depending on their several kinds: the law which God has eternally imposed upon Himself to follow in His own works, the law which He has made for his creatures, the law for natural agents and forces of nature, the law which the heavenly angels must obey, the law which the light of reason shows men must obey by virtue of their humanity, the law agreed upon for the ordering of multitudes and political societies, the law of particular nations, the law concerning the fellowship of all nations, and finally the law supernaturally revealed by God. This book might have been more popular and more accessible to the masses if it had merely extolled the force of laws and the necessity of good laws, and had railed against the evils of those who attack them. However, this kind of rhetoric is more liable to stir up passions than to build up understanding of the issues in question. I have therefore gone off the beaten path and chosen a way that is, though less easy, more useful for our purposes. Lest anyone should wonder what the point of this whole argument is, my goal is to show how, like every good and perfect gift, so also this gift of good and perfect law comes down from the Father of lights (Jas. 1:17); to teach men why just and reasonable laws have so much force and use in the world; and to show them a method for taking the laws under debate, and tracing them back to their first principles, so that we can better recognize in particular commands whether they are reasonable, just, and righteous or not. Can we truly understand or properly judge anything until the first causes and principles behind it are revealed? As wise men say, going back to the first axioms of any science is the best way to proceed in any sort of knowledge.[1] Since our question has to do with ecclesiastical laws, it is clearly necessary for us to consider all these different classes of law, since all play a role in grounding and giving force to ecclesiastical laws, though not all in an equally obvious manner (which is why many have failed to understand the force of these laws).

(2.) It is much easier to teach men by law what they should do, than to teach them how to rightly think of the law. Everyone must do the former, while none but the wisest and most judicious of men can do the latter. Indeed, the wisest are always the first to admit that to soundly judge laws is the weightiest thing a man can undertake.[2] If, however, we must judge the laws under which we live, then first let the eternal law be always before our eyes. It is of

---

[1] Aristotle, *Physics* 1.1 [184a].

[2] Aristotle, *Nicomachean Ethics* 10 [1181a].

CONCLUSION

such great weight and consequence that in religious minds it fosters a dutiful estimation of all laws which benefit mankind. There can be no doubt that good laws are, so to speak, copied out of the tables of the high everlasting law, just as the book of that law says, "By me kings reign and princes decree justice" (Prov. 8:15). This is not because men look at this eternal law as if they were looking at a book and determine their laws accordingly. Rather, this is because when the laws rulers make are righteous, the eternal law is at work in them and, in a way, is revealing itself to the world by these laws. We do not always perceive the goodness of laws, but since in any good thing there may be much that we do not yet discern, we should take care lest we hastily and unjustly condemn that which God has ordained, bringing dishonor to Him before whom we all profess submission and awe. Surely the laws must be very bad indeed, if our impudent accusations are to be justified! The chief cause of this error is ignorance of how lower laws are derived from the supreme or eternal law.

(3.) The first who bear the stamp of this law are natural agents. When considering laws that regard human actions, such laws of nature may seem irrelevant, but even in spiritual and supernatural actions, the principles of merely natural actions inevitably continue to apply. For example, what can be more essential to men's salvation than our belief that Christ has bound himself to His Church? What can make us more sure of Christ's love for His Church than the knowledge of that mystical union which makes the Church as close to Christ as any one part of His flesh is to another? What greater proof do we have that He will protect His Church than if an inviolable law so decrees? And in proof of this, the Apostle cites a law which applies not only to Christ, but also to us and to all natural creatures: "for no man ever hated his own flesh; but nourisheth and cherisheth it, even as Christ also the church" (Eph. 5:29)? The principles of that law which guides natural agents therefore also apply to the moral and even spiritual actions of men, and thus to all sorts of laws affecting men.

(4.) Regarding the law that governs angels, their heavenly service is not so dissimilar to our earthly service that it can shed no light for us; on the contrary, knowledge of this celestial law informs our practice here on earth. Would angels call themselves fellow-servants with the sons of men to the same Lord unless there were some kind of law common to us both? Is not their obedience an example and a spur to ours? Or would the Apostles, whenever they describe the saints joined in a spiritual union, so often say that the angels are delighted with our worship, unless this worship bears some resemblance to that which angels already do in heaven (1 Pet. 1:12; Eph. 3:10; 1 Tim. 5:21)? Indeed, the Apostle goes so far as to say that even in the outward orders of the church which merely have to do with decency, we should have regard for the angels (1 Cor. 11:10). In short, we must not imagine that the law of angels is completely irrelevant to the affairs of the Church of God.

(5.) As for our careful definition of human laws (that is, of how men discover what reason obligates them to do and how it guides them to choose in indifferent matters) as well as our care in distinguishing those laws which concern men as individuals, or men in civil or spiritual societies, or the fellowship between whole nations, and the laws which

CONCLUSION

Scripture contains on each of these matters—we have done all this to make clear that, just as man's actions are of many different sorts, so the laws of men must be distinguished accordingly. The actions of men are of many kinds—some are natural, some rational, some supernatural, some political, and some ecclesiastical—and if we do not treat each in its own proper manner, we will be sure to fall into confusion.

As a matter of fact, our opponents in this dispute have built their case on just such a confusion. They rightly maintain that God must be glorified in all things and that men's actions cannot glorify Him unless they are based on His laws. However, they are mistaken to think that the only law which God has appointed for this is Scripture. What we do naturally, such as breathing, sleeping, and moving, displays the glory of God just as natural agents do, even if we do not have any express purpose in mind, but act for the most part unconsciously. Another law governs our rational and moral actions, a law by which we glorify God in a way that no other creature under man can do, since other creatures do not have the discernment to know what sorts of things they do, and as a result they can neither accuse nor excuse themselves. Men do both, as the Apostle says (Rom. 2:15). Indeed, those men who have no written law to show them what is good or evil have the universal law of mankind, the law of reason, written in their hearts, which God has given them as a rule by which to judge. The law of reason teaches men in part how to honor God as their Creator, but we are taught by divine law how to glorify Him in such a way that He may be our everlasting Savior. This divine law both makes certain the truth of the law of reason and supplies what is lacking in it;

therefore in moral actions, the divine law greatly helps the law of reason in guiding man's life, but in supernatural matters, it alone guides us.

We can go further: if man is to live in a public society with others, then he needs another sort of law, whether that society be civil or ecclesiastical. Even though the laws of nature and reason are necessary here too, something beyond them is also necessary, namely human and positive law, along with the law governing dealings between nations. For this reason, the law of God has likewise said, "Let every soul be in subjection to the higher powers" (Rom. 13:1). The public power of all societies is above every soul within them, and the purpose of this power is to give laws to those under it. We must obey these laws, unless sufficient reason proves that the Law of Reason or of God commands the opposite. After all, unless our private and only probable judgments can be overruled by publicly-determined laws, we would lose all possibility of sociable life in this world. Where can we find a better example of this turmoil than our own time? How is it that at this present day we are so beset by strifes and dissensions and the Church is so torn over church government? Doubtless, if men had been willing to learn how many laws govern their actions and what the true force of each law is, all these controversies might have died on the very day they were first brought forth.

(6.) It has often been truly said that those who are otherwise the best of men are not necessarily the best men when it comes to their membership in society.[3] The reason

---

[3] Aristotle, *Nicomachean Ethics* 5.3 [1129b].

CONCLUSION

for this is that the law by which we measure men's actions as moral agents is quite different from that which considers them as parts of a political body. There are many men who are very upright and commendable as individuals, and yet when they are in a society with others they are simply cannot perform the duties required of them. Indeed, I am convinced that the men with whom we are striving in this case are the sort whose betters among men might scarcely be found, if only they did not live among men, but lived off in a wilderness on their own. The reason that their dispositions are so ill-suited to their society is because they have not understood what roles the different kinds of laws should have in their actions. If there is a question either about church government or about conformity between churches or about ceremonies, offices, powers, and jurisdictions in our church, they begin by framing a rule of interpretation that seems likely, and whatever conclusion this yields, they think themselves bound to practice. They then labor mightily to advocate this, whatever any law of man decides to the contrary. Thus by following the law of private reason where the law of public reason should prevail, they become disturbers of the peace.

(7.) So that we might accustom men's minds to better distinguishing between the different kinds of laws and how they apply to us, depending on the kind and quality of our actions, let us offer a concrete example of an area of conduct where they all apply. We need go no further than to consider something which is familiar to all of us: our food.

What things are and are not fit to eat, we judge by our senses. Nor do we need any other law to tell us so besides that faculty which we have in common with beasts. However, when we consider food as a gift which God has provided for all living things, the law of reason demands that we be thankful to Him from whose hands we have it. Furthermore, lest appetite for food should lead us to gluttony, we ought to obey the law of reason that teaches moderation regarding food and drink. The divine law of Scripture teaches the same thing, as we have previously shown it does in all parts of moral duty to which we are all bound as far as the life to come is concerned.

However, we also have foods with spiritual, religious, and supernatural uses, just as the Jews did. They had their Passover lambs and offerings; we have our bread and wine in the Eucharist, which could only have been instituted by divine law.

Now, since we live in society, the commonwealth in which we live may and does require certain things concerning food. These are the sort of laws which we would not need to obey otherwise, but since we are members of a commonwealth in which they have authority, we are obliged to respect and obey them.

Indeed, the same is true sometimes of ecclesiastical laws. Unless we want to be authors of division in the church, our private discretion which might lead us in a different direction otherwise must here submit to being guided by what the public judgment of the church has thought to be better. The words of Zonaras ought to be remembered in this case: though fasts are good, even good things should be done in a good and beneficial manner, and he that violates the orders of the holy fathers in his fasting (which were the positive laws of the church) must be plainly told that good things cease to be good when they are not per-

CONCLUSION

formed in a good manner.[4]

Here men's private fancies must give place to the higher judgment of the church which is in authority a mother to them. In this way, whole churches have been subject to laws concerning food for the sake of their fellowship with other churches, even if individual churches might have thought the opposite was more beneficial. An example of such can be found in the Council of Jerusalem's decision regarding abstinence from things strangled and from blood, which was based on the need for orderly fellowship between Gentile and Jewish churches.[5]

Thus we see how a single thing is dealt with in many ways by many different laws, and that to judge the actions of men by any single law would confuse the admirable order by which God has disposed every law in nature and degree, one distinct from another.

(8.) Therefore, we may end here. We must acknowledge of Law that her seat lies in the bosom of God, that her voice is the harmony of the world, and that all things in heaven and earth do her homage. The least feels her care, the greatest is not exempt from her power. Both angels and

---

[4] Zonaras on Apostolic canon 66, in *Patrologiae cursus completus*, Series Graeca, ed. Jacques-Paul Migne (Paris: J.-P. Migne, 1844-1891), 137:172.

[5] Note that Hooker is here operating on the assumption that this prohibition, rooted in Lev. 17:13–14, should be understood as part of the ceremonial law, abrogated in principle in the New Testament (thus an example of divine positive law only temporarily in force). Accordingly, he takes its continuation in Acts 15 by the Apostles as an example of church authorities essentially promulgating a human positive law that was likewise of temporary effect. Of course, it is also possible to interpret the passage in Acts 15 as implying that the prohibition was not, after all, part of the temporary ceremonial law, but an example of an abiding moral law of the Old Covenant.

men and creatures of any sort, each in their different ways, admire her with uniform consent as the mother of their peace and joy.

ABOUT THE AUTHOR

Richard Hooker (1553/4—1600) was the pre-eminent theological writer of the Elizabethan church, and many would say in the entire history of the Church of England. He achieved this status despite holding no high office during his life and authoring only one major work, *The Laws of Ecclesiastical Polity*, which remained incomplete at his untimely death. Trained at Oxford under the moderate Puritan theologian John Rainolds, Hooker went on, after a high-profile conflict with the presbyterian leader Walter Travers, to undertake a systematic criticism of radical Puritan theology and practice, offering the most influential defense of the Church of England (not yet conceived of as "Anglican" in a theologically distinctive sense, but simply as English Protestant).

ABOUT THE DAVENANT TRUST

The Davenant Trust supports the renewal of Christian wisdom for the contemporary church. It seeks to sponsor historical scholarship at the intersection of the church and academy, build networks of friendship and collaboration within the Reformed and evangelical world, and equip the saints with time-tested resources for faithful public witness.

We are a nonprofit organization supported by your tax-deductible gifts. Learn more about us, and donate, at www.davenanttrust.org.